T0274843

WORLD WAR I
OKLAHOMA

WORLD WAR I
OKLAHOMA

James P. Gregory Jr.

THE
History
PRESS

Published by The History Press
Charleston, SC
www.historypress.com

Copyright © 2024 by James P. Gregory Jr.
All rights reserved

First published 2024

Manufactured in the United States

ISBN 9781467155588

Library of Congress Control Number: 2023945796

Notice: The information in this book is true and complete to the best of our knowledge. It is offered without guarantee on the part of the author or The History Press. The author and The History Press disclaim all liability in connection with the use of this book.

All rights reserved. No part of this book may be reproduced or transmitted in any form whatsoever without prior written permission from the publisher except in the case of brief quotations embodied in critical articles and reviews.

CONTENTS

Prologue. Mexican Border Service   7

1. Preparing for War   11
2. Resistance   21
3. Life on the Homefront   35
4. Native American Participation   45
5. Flu Epidemic   51
6. Oklahoma Doughboys   63

Notes   85
About the Author   95

Prologue

MEXICAN BORDER SERVICE

On March 9, 1916, Francisco "Pancho" Villa attacked the town of Columbus, New Mexico, and killed eighteen Americans. Villa sought retaliation against the United States for supporting his opponent Álvaro Obregón during the ongoing civil war in Mexico. A detachment of the 13th Cavalry Regiment is presumed to have been the main target of the raid for Villa to capture weapons and supplies to continue his war. Although the attack was ultimately repulsed, the town burned to the ground, and Mexican forces captured over one hundred mules and horses. This attack shocked the American public and launched them into action on their southern border.

Villa had targeted Columbus for its small size and remote location despite being adjacent to Camp Furlong, which housed a squadron from the 13th Cavalry consisting of around 275 soldiers. However, the camp did not have adequate housing, so many of the officers quartered in Columbus. Early in the morning of March 9, around five hundred Villistas (as Villa's men came to be called) organized small parties and crossed into the United States. One group rode toward Camp Furlong, while the other entered Columbus. At 4:00 a.m., the Mexicans attacked both locations.

In Camp Furlong, the cavalrymen managed to quickly recover from their surprise and put up a formidable defense armed with whatever they could grab. Even the cooks joined the fight with kitchen utensils and pots of boiling water. In town, the Villistas managed to enter the hotel and murdered several townspeople while setting fire to the surrounding buildings. The Mexicans then looted and burned private residences. After an intense shootout lasting almost two hours, Villa's force retreated to the Mexican border. The American cavalry pursued the invaders into Mexico and engaged them repeatedly. After pushing almost fifteen miles into Mexico, the Americans ran low on ammunition and water; therefore, they turned back and returned to Camp Furlong.

Although Villa successfully surprised the American forces around Columbus, the raid ultimately failed as a military operation. Villa's forces suffered significant losses of around one hundred dead and around thirty captured. In comparison, the United States cavalry suffered eight killed and five wounded, while twenty civilians were killed. The response of President Woodrow Wilson was swift due to the tremendous pressure to act with an upcoming presidential election. He quickly mobilized troops to the border and authorized the expedition into northern Mexico. This major undertaking, termed the "Punitive Expedition," required tremendous effort in logistics and changes in military doctrine thanks to the U.S. Army's relatively small size in the spring of 1916. American forces had experience in fighting small guerrilla forces in the tropics, but an expedition into Mexico would require large, multiunit coordination on a scale the army had not seen.

By March 15, 1917, President Woodrow Wilson had authorized Brigadier General John J. Pershing to raise an expedition into Chihuahua, Mexico, to kill or capture Pancho Villa. Pershing assembled nearly 4,800 troops around Columbus and entered the Mexican countryside. This force would eventually grow to around 10,000 regular army troops and approximately 110,000 National Guardsmen who patrolled the American border thanks to a patriotic fervor after the attack. Led by Apache scouts or local Mexicans, the army covered a large swath of desolate terrain. This endeavor gave the United States an opportunity to test out new methods of warfare, such as the use of airplanes and trucks instead of horses. This eleven-month expedition failed to even spot Pancho Villa, but it trained thousands of soldiers in large field operations. While seeing little action, the troops on the border received training that would bolster the army for its eventual war against Germany.[1]

The crisis on the Mexican border strengthened American readiness with the National Defense Act of 1916. In response to Pancho Villa and the ongoing war in Europe, the act increased the size of the regular army and the National Guard while also increasing federal control over the guard. To aid the army marching through Mexico, Wilson ordered the National Guard from three states into federal service on May 9, 1916. By July 4, the National Guards from fourteen states served along the Mexican border.

Company E, 1ˢᵗ Oklahoma Infantry. *Author's collection.*

Due to the large presence of troops along the border, no other incursions into the United States occurred, meaning most guardsmen saw no military action. However, the training the guardsmen received proved invaluable. It hardened the troops and gave officers much-needed experience in handling troops in the field. By the time America entered World War I, many of the guard units had already been trained and equipped.

Among the National Guard units stationed on the border were those of Texas and Oklahoma, with Texas being mobilized first. The Oklahoma National Guard was one of the country's smaller organizations, consisting of the 1ˢᵗ Infantry Regiment; the 1ˢᵗ and 2ⁿᵈ Cavalry troops; the Field Hospital; the Ambulance Corps; the Regimental Infirmary; and the Engineer Company. Most of the Oklahoma guardsmen were stationed in San Benito and Donna, Texas. The 1ˢᵗ Oklahoma Infantry formed part of a brigade in the regular army under Colonel Robert L. Bullard.[2]

The excitement and patriotic fervor that brought many Oklahomans to join the guard quickly faded under the monotony of life on the Mexican border. During their tenure, only a minor clash with Mexican bandits and raiders gave relief from the routine of drill and marches. The Oklahoma guardsmen did, however, find some entertainment through their culture, as many of the Native American troops would perform war dances for the men. Fortunately, their service on the border did not last too long, as they had served their purpose by early 1917. In February, the last of the Oklahoma guardsmen returned to Oklahoma and were released from active duty.

In March, the Texas National Guard demobilized but was cut short in late March by the War Department, which suspended deactivation and instead recalled some guard units back into federal service. The war in Europe had taken a turn, and it appeared inevitable that the United States would be sucked into it. The National Guards, including Oklahoma, commenced mobilization in early April until April 6, 1917, when Congress declared war on Germany. To create their new army, the United States began to mobilize the regular army, National Guard and national army, which consisted of draftees. For Oklahoma and Texas, their National Guards combined to form the 36th Division and would go on to serve with distinction in France.

Chapter 1

PREPARING FOR WAR

As the country prepared for war, the State of Oklahoma began to organize to do its part in supplying men for service. The state set in motion the tools for its draft in May 1917 and continued until January 1919. A majority of the men who worked for the draft boards volunteered their time as a service to the war effort, an undertaking that required six hours a day, six days a week. Some even claimed to have worked eight to eighteen hours. The State of Oklahoma took a hard stance against avoiding the draft and due to this had some of the highest rates of registration in the country. By the end of 1918, the state boasted a total of 473,231 registered men, which comprised 37,563 African Americans, around 5,000 Native Americans and nearly 9,000 foreign-born immigrants.[3]

FORT SILL

In response to the United States' expansion into the West and removal of Native American tribes into Indian Territory, which would later become Oklahoma, many forts were constructed throughout the region. On January 8, 1869, Major General Philip H. Sheridan began the construction of Camp Wichita, which would later be called Fort Sill. At the end of the nineteenth century, the military's need to police Native Americans fell away, and many of the camps closed their doors. Fort Sill languished and almost dissolved, but a growing number of field artillery units and addition of aircraft in 1915 gave it a new purpose.

Opposite: Observation balloon at Fort Sill, 1918. *Author's collection.*

Above: Plane at Fort Sill, 1918. *Author's collection.*

Fort Sill became the birthplace of combat aviation for the United States military. The presence of field artillery meant that the army could practice aerial reconnaissance of field positions and the use of aerial photography. During the 1916 border crisis, most of the aircraft from Fort Sill traveled to Texas and then into Mexico, where they performed a variety of tasks from reconnaissance to delivering mail. In August 1917, Henry Post Army Airfield was established at Fort Sill to train aerial observers to work alongside field artillery, which would find great success in France. One of the units, the 1st Aero Squadron, was commanded by Captain Benjamin Foulois, who had been trained by the Wright brothers.[4]

Alongside airplanes, the army added balloon squadrons to Fort Sill, with Company A, 1st Balloon Squadron, arriving on September 5, 1917. These, too, served as aerial observers for the artillery and trained at the field's Balloon Corps Training School. During the war, around eighty-nine companies received training at the school, with thirty-three of them deploying to France for service. The men who trained for this job found themselves in a dangerous unit that would be an easy target for enemy aircraft. The balloons would be tethered to the ground and winched from trucks on the ground. Filled with hydrogen, the balloons were susceptible to catching fire. Operating at heights of 4,300 feet meant that if they were attacked, survival would be difficult, so the army supplied observers with parachutes.[5]

CAMP DONIPHAN

Alongside Fort Sill, the army built Camp Doniphan to train artillery units. Named after the Mexican-American War hero Alexander Doniphan, the camp would also provide basic training to thousands of soldiers from Oklahoma, Kansas and Missouri during the war. The nature of the environment and the hot desert climate of southwestern Oklahoma combined with the living conditions in tents to make a hell on earth for many of the men who trained at Camp Doniphan.

The camp became home to the 35th Infantry Division, made up of the Kansas and Missouri National Guards. One of the most notable of these soldiers who spent time at Camp Doniphan was future president Harry S. Truman, who ran the regimental canteen from September 1917 to March 1918. While at the camp, the men began to get restless with their surroundings, so a trolley line from the camp to Lawton, Oklahoma, provided some means of entertainment while on leave. The Knights of Columbus and YMCA also set up canteens at Camp Doniphan to offer a relief from the monotony of their surroundings. Recalling his time at the camp, an unnamed soldier who worked with the Knights of Columbus wrote of his comrades:

> These men begged for overseas service in order to help exterminate the Hun, and were denied. They were kept here to fight other battles, namely; rattlesnakes, tarantulas, horned toads, lizards, hurricanes, sand, and weather of unbearable heat, throughout the summer; snow, rain, sleet, hail, and weather of bitterest coldness, throughout the winter. They have done their bit.[6]

Knights of Columbus workers at Camp Doniphan. *Author's collection.*

Practice trenches at Camp Doniphan. *Author's collection.*

For those unfortunate enough to be stationed at Camp Doniphan, their memories would not be pleasant. After the war, Camp Doniphan dissolved, and the training of field artillery became the responsibility of Fort Sill.

36TH DIVISION

Those who served in the Oklahoma National Guard found themselves federalized and placed into the 36th Division. Made up of the Oklahoma and Texas National Guards, the 36th Division adopted the symbol of an arrowhead with a *T* in the center to represent both states. Originally designated the 15th Division, in July 1917, they changed to the 36th. In strength, the division was composed of:

Headquarters
36th Military Police Company
131st Machine Gun Battalion
71st Infantry Brigade
   141st Regiment
   142nd Regiment
   132nd Machine Gun Battalion
72nd Infantry Brigade
   143rd Regiment
   144th Regiment
   133rd Machine Gun Battalion
61st Field Artillery Brigade
   131st Field Artillery
   132nd Field Artillery
   133rd Field Artillery
   111th Trench Mortar Battery
   111th Ammunition Train
111th Engineer Regiment
111th Field Signal Battalion
111th Supply Train
111th Sanitary Train
   Ambulance Companies 141, 142, 143, 144
   Field Hospitals 141, 142, 143, 144

The 36th Division trained at Camp Travis, Texas, until traveling overseas in July 1918. Upon arriving in France, the division traveled to Bar-sur-Aube Training Area. Here the men familiarized themselves with the French countryside and trained with the latest American weapons and tactics. They remained in this training area until September 26, 1918. However, the 61st Artillery Brigade would not accompany the division and instead remained in training at Coetquidan. They would never see any combat action. Likewise, the 111th Engineers were detached from the 36th Division and assigned to the American First Army as corps engineers on September 11, 1918. They would remain with the First Army throughout the war, participating in the St. Mihiel and Meuse-Argonne Offensives.

Without their artillery or engineers, the 36th Division moved to the Pocancy Area to serve alongside the Reserves of the French army. On October 3rd, the division transferred over to the Fourth French Army under General Henri Gouraud to fight alongside the American 2nd Division at Blanc Mont Ridge. Here the 36th Division would experience the hell of war and cement their legacy.

On October 4, the 71st Brigade moved to the Somme-Suippe area and transferred to the 21st Corps French Army the next day. On the night of the sixth, the 71st Brigade relieved the Second Division southeast of St. Etienne. On October 8, 1918, the 71st Brigade launched its attack between St. Etienne and Madeah Farm with the 141st Infantry on the right and the 142nd Infantry on the left. For the next few days, the brigade clashed against fierce German opposition but managed to capture around six hundred prisoners and broke the German resistance north of Blanc Mont.

On October 10, the 36th relieved the 2nd Division but kept the 2nd Engineers and 12th, 15th and 17th Field Artillery Regiments to support their continued advances. By the next day, the 36th Division had pushed the Germans back to the Aisne River and taken up positions just south of the river. Here they remained until being relieved by the 22nd French Division on October 27. They then moved to the Conde-en-Barrois Area as part of the reserves for the First American Army. The division then spent the period from November 4 through the armistice equipping and training replacements.

Despite only a few days of combat, the division suffered 2,601 casualties, including 574 killed and 94 missing. For their efforts, the division received 2 Medals of Honor, 30 Distinguished Service Crosses and 129 Croix de Guerre.[7] Once the war ended, the 36th Division spent the next few months in France on occupation duties. The 36th Division returned home to the United States, where it was deactivated in July 1919.

90TH DIVISION

For those drafted from Oklahoma and Texas, the 90th Division of the National Army became their division. Known as the "Tough Ombres" the division wore a patch that combined an 'O' and 'T' to represent both states. In strength, the division was composed of:

Headquarters
315th Military Police Company
343rd Machine Gun Battalion
179th Infantry Brigade
   357th Regiment
   358th Regiment
   344th Machine Gun Battalion
180th Infantry Brigade
   359th Regiment
   360th Regiment
   345th Machine Gun Battalion
165th Field Artillery Brigade
   343rd Field Artillery
   344th Field Artillery
   345th Field Artillery
   315th Trench Mortar Battery
   315th Ammunition Train
315th Engineer Regiment
315th Field Signal Battalion
315th Supply Train
315th Sanitary Train
   Ambulance Companies 357, 358, 359, 360
   Field Hospitals 357, 358, 359, 360

The 90th Division formed on August 25, 1917, at Camp Travis, Texas. Regular army officers turned drafted men into a formidable fighting force. The 179th Brigade became the Oklahoma Brigade, while the 180th Brigade represented Texas. In June 1918, the division began to move toward New York for their trip overseas. The division traveled to France from June 13 to July 6. The 90th Division eventually collected in the Aignay-le-Duc training area north of Dijon, France, in the Cote-d'Or Mountains. Much like the 36th Division, the 165th Artillery Brigade became detached and billeted in Camp

90th Division insignia. *Author's collection.*

Hunt at Le Courneau training area. They would not rejoin the division until after the armistice. The division trained until August 15, when they moved to support the St. Mihiel Offensive.

The 90th Division relieved the 1st Division north of Toul. On September 12, the American forces began their advance to cut off the St. Mihiel Salient. Due to thickly strewn barbed wire and fortified German defensive positions, the 358th Regiment experienced great difficulties in their advance, suffering heavy losses, while the 357th and 360th Regiments easily obtained their objectives. However, due to the determination of the men, all objectives were taken by 2:00 p.m.

On September 13, the Germans counterattacked but failed against the 357th Regiment. Meanwhile, the 360th Infantry attacked and captured the Bois-le-Pretre and the Norroy Quarries. On September 14, the 358th Infantry advanced to Les Quatre Chemins. The advance of the 90th Division continued until September 16, when the stabilization of the salient took place. It was up to the 90th to hold their positions until relief arrived on October 10. Constant artillery bombardment by the Germans continued to kill and wound men in what they termed "Death Valley," but the Americans held their territory. On September 23, a small group from the 357th Regiment successfully raided the German trenches, capturing five prisoners. The 90th Division held their territory until being relieved by the 7th Division during the period of October 8–10.

Their rest would not last long, as they reentered the line on the Meuse-Argonne front on October 21. The 90th was tasked with straightening out the line between the Bois des Rappes and Bois de Bantheville, which included the towns of Bantheville and Bourrut. On October 23, the 357th Infantry advanced forward and captured Bantheville and Bourrut through a terrific artillery barrage. On the twenty-fifth, the Germans attempted a counterattack, which was quickly defeated.

On November 1, the 360th Infantry pushed forward through terrific machine gun and artillery barrages and managed to capture Grand Carre Farm, Hill 300, and Hill 278. By the end of the day, they had captured all objectives. The next morning, on November 2, the 360th Infantry pushed forward once more and captured the Bois de Roux and Hill 321. That same day, the 359th Infantry captured Villers-devant-Dun and held off a German counterattack. Through these two days of fighting, the 180th Brigade captured 807 German prisoners. November 3 would provide the 179th Brigade its opportunity to further its storied legacy. However, once the men began their advance, they found no resistance. The Germans had retreated across the Meuse River in the night, which meant the Oklahoma Brigade easily captured all their objectives and prepared to cross the Meuse River.

For the next six days, the men dug in and waited for their orders to continue chasing the Germans. Finally, on November 9, the division received orders to cross the Meuse on the repaired bridge at Sassey. The 90th Division began crossing immediately and took up positions to continue their advance. On November 10, just hours before the armistice would end hostilities, the 90th Division engaged in severe and costly engagements. The 358th Infantry had the objective of Stenay while the 357th was to take Jardinelle Farm, which overlooked the town of Baalon. Both attacks successfully captured their objectives, but by the end of the day, the 90th Division had suffered 34 killed in action and 183 wounded, just hours before the war ended.

With the signing of the armistice on November 11, 1918, hostilities ceased. However, the 90th would not be going home. Instead, they marched into Germany as part of the Army of Occupation. The division billeted in and around the German town of Bernkastel-Kues, where it remained until May 1919, when the men began to sail home.[8]

Chapter 2

RESISTANCE

GREEN CORN REBELLION

By 1917, the Socialist Party of Oklahoma claimed the support of 20 percent of the state. Since the state's wealth generally fell with the railroads and oil companies, radicalism found a home among the many impoverished farmers who operated small farms around the state. Anger at a growing number of wealthy landholders who adopted shady practices to acquire more land and the falling of crop prices in the early years of World War I meant that discontent was coming to a head. The Socialist Party preached an expansion of public domain and cooperative markets, and this drove around thirty-five thousand farmers to join the Working Class Union (WCU) at the beginning of World War I in 1914.

By 1916, the WCU claimed a membership of almost twenty thousand in eastern Oklahoma.[9] Almost half of the tenant farmers in Oklahoma were young, between the age of twenty-five and thirty-three.[10] This became the main point of contention with the United States' entry into the war in 1917. To create an army large enough to compete with the German military, the federal government passed the Selective Service Act, which would begin a draft to increase the size of the military. This required all men between the ages of twenty-one and forty-five to register for the draft by June 5, 1917. For many of these young farmers, the possibility of being pulled away from their farms and families surely meant failure of their crop and the loss of their home. Anger and discomfort quickly grew among the tenant farmers in central Oklahoma, so they decided to end the war on their own terms.

In August 1917, hundreds of farmers from all walks of life—White, Black and Native American—gathered at the farm of a Socialist named John Spears in Sasakwa, Oklahoma. They planned on marching to Washington, D.C., and demanding an end to the war, through violence if necessary. They would sustain themselves on barbecued beef and roasted green corn, which would give their resistance the name Green Corn Rebellion. Approximately eight hundred armed rebels—some have argued for a much smaller number—began to amass near the adjoining borders of Pontotoc, Seminole and Hughes Counties, in southeastern Oklahoma, and prepared for their long march.[11]

On August 3, 1917, they began their violent march by cutting telegraph lines and burning bridges in their rural communities to prevent the authorities from learning of their movements. However, the plans were immediately transmitted to the local authorities by an informer. In response to this news, Oklahoma governor Robert Lee Williams ordered Captain L.E. Donahue of Troop A Cavalry to take a squad of ten sharpshooters to Seminole County to stop this resistance. The men brought "4,000 rounds of ammunition and extra arms" to Holdenville, Oklahoma, where they found around 500 to 600 armed citizens to protect the town. At midnight, a special train arrived from Okmulgee and Henryetta with 300 men under U.S. marshal Enlow. Enlow took a posse to Wewoka, while Donahue took his men to Sasakwa. Sheriffs from Seminole, Pittsburg and Pontotoc Counties also joined Donahue with automobiles of more men, which brought Donahue's posse up to 1,500 men. They spread throughout the countryside and managed to arrest 19 men and release 9 men they found tied to trees for refusing to join the rebellion. Donahue's men did not fire any weapons in their roundup.[12]

Enlow's posse, on the other hand, engaged in combat with the rebels. Upon seeing "hundreds of determined citizens from Seminole, Hughes, Pontotoc, and Pott County" alongside state troops, the rebels scattered throughout the countryside. The posse engaged a small group in a short battle in which Wallace Cargille, an alleged leader, was killed and the others captured. Over the next few days, the posses continued to chase the rebels throughout the county and captured many of them.[13] After only a few days, the Green Corn Rebellion was ended with 3 people killed, which included Wallace Cargille and Clifford Clark, a Black tenant farmer, and more than 400 arrested. Of those, 150 were convicted and received federal prison terms of up to ten years.[14]

The Green Corn Rebellion proved to be the final nail in the coffin for the Socialist Party of Oklahoma, which took the blame for the rebellion alongside the Industrial Workers of the World (IWW), despite the WCU being the organization most of the tenant farmers belonged to. Regardless of where the true blame fell, the public backlash against Socialists in the states forced the Socialist Party to disband and spurred violent patriotism throughout the state in response to anyone who refused to support the draft.

CREEK DRAFT REBELLION

On June 6, 1918, the *Daily Oklahoman* ran the headline "200 CREEKS GO ON WARPATH OVER DRAFTING OF YOUTHS; 3 WHITES RUMORED KILLED."[15] The story of an Indian rebellion ran in newspapers across the country from Oregon to New York. In the midst of World War I, the United States found itself in a domestic open conflict with the Creek Nation in Henryetta, Oklahoma. However, by the time the article ran on June 6, the rebellion had begun and ended without any violence from the Creek Nation.

On June 5, 1918, a group of approximately fifty Creek men, women and children, including Black Creeks, gathered at the Old Hickory Stomping Grounds in the Salem District, six miles southeast of Henryetta.[16] The reason for this meeting varies in the reports from the establishment of a Grand Army of the Republic post, a discussion of war support or a debate on Creek Nation politics.[17] During this meeting, a group of Black Creeks went to "Elmer Fowler's store to buy supplies for their gathering." When the group attempted to purchase wheat flour, Fowler informed them that they could not buy any without a "flour card" issued by the county food administrator.[18] H.C. Fellows, the local food administrator of Henryetta, had recently announced the new rule. In fact, it was not published in the *Henryetta Standard* until June 6, the day after the altercation. The rule read in part, "No one living in your district can buy flour, bread, crackers, macaroni, breakfast food, or pastry containing wheat flour, without presenting to the dealer a card with your name to it." To ensure that the shopkeepers followed the new rules, the Food Administration threatened, "If a merchant sells without actually punching out of the card, at the time of the sale, the pounds purchased, no jobber will be allowed to sell him hereafter." The cards also served to find unpatriotic citizens because "many will patriotically get along with less, it's the unpatriotic, selfish ones we are after."[19] The frustrated group of Creeks "declared to Fowler that he might just as well sell them the flour, for they would come and take it by force if he did not."[20] Fowler would not sell the group any flour, so they returned to the gathering distraught.

This new grievance with the war effort sparked discussion at the meeting of discontent with the United States government. The Creeks remarked that "we give to Red Cross, buy Liberty Bonds, are taken to war, and are refused flour, yet we can't vote."[21] This discussion likely expanded to other issues such as the drafting of Native American soldiers. The status of Native citizenship created confusion in registering for the draft. Native American men had to register, but only those possessing citizenship were liable for the draft. "Many noncitizen Indians believed that they were exempt from registering because they were not citizens."[22] This uncertainty understandably irritated and angered Native groups and created a point of contention between them and the white, overzealously patriotic communities. During these discussions, Ellen Perryman, a prominent Creek woman, supposedly spoke out against the United States government.

The isolated farmers in the Salem section viewed the large numbers of assembled Creeks with alarm and inquired about the "bitterness in the minds of those people."[23] At around nine o'clock in the evening, a farmer, identified only as Morrison, brought reports to Henryetta "that the Creeks had attacked two white farmers" and were "inflamed by the drafting of about 60 of their youths."[24] Accordingly, the Henryetta Home Guard assembled, loaded into a number of vehicles and rushed to the scene. Lieutenant Ray Wise and Lieutenant Lincoln led the "expeditionary force" of fifty men.[25] A local reporter, Jack Carter, heard of the "uprising" and immediately wired newspapers for funds to travel to the scene. He then followed the troops into the battle awaiting them.[26]

Upon the Home Guard's arrival, they fired shots to disrupt the gathering. The sudden attack caused the women and children "to scatter in the woods."[27] Lieutenant Ray Wise later stated that "he found between twenty and thirty people assembled." The Creeks explained that "their meeting was to settle some of their affairs, and that there would be no trouble caused. They agreed to disperse when morning came."[28] While at the Stomping Grounds, Jack Carter entered the house of Jeff Francis and interviewed Ellen Perryman, who was distraught over the sudden attack. She "refused to talk about the purported uprising but kept on talking of how the Indians have been treated by the white people."[29] Perryman, according to Carter, made many crude anti-government comments during their dialogue. He claimed she "severely attacked the Government of the United States" and referred to soldiers as "the yellow-legged S. of B." Perhaps the most egregious claim Carter makes is her parting words: "To Hell with the United States, Damn President Wilson, and I would not wipe my ass on the Stars and Stripes."[30] Carter concluded from this interview that Perryman spoke out to the group of gathered Creeks. However, he never collected any evidence proving that she gave a speech. In fact, Francis later testified that Perryman "did not make any speech to the Indians but seems as though she had intended to."[31]

To the Creeks assembled, the sudden ringing of gunfire and presence of the Home Guard terrified them and secured their distrust of the local government. Tulsay, a prominent Creek, sent a telegram the next morning requesting assistance for the "hostilities on us" as the Creeks found themselves "in a terrible condition…outside people caused weeping."[32] Ellen Perryman also sent a telegram on June 7, stating that at dark, a "mob of people threw guns on us scattering women and children even threatened me.…They always hated Indians. Pleading for help. Please notify authority."[33] The "Creek Draft Rebellion" had no violence from the side of the Creek.

Despite their show of force, the troops found no armed resistance. Lieutenant Wise reported that upon their arrival, "no one was armed nor offered any resistance."[34] After only an hour, the Home Guard and Carter returned to Henryetta at 10:30 p.m. Carter quickly wrote up his story of a rebellion led by an anti-government Creek woman and sent it out to various newspapers. In the local area, rumors spread about the conflict that had taken place as the Home Guard attempted to quell the uprising. Newspapers reported a fight upon the arrival of the troops, stating, "Many shots were heard." This resistance, paired with the news that a woman named Ellen Perryman led the rebels and spread sedition among the Creek, quickly inspired local law enforcement to gather a posse in order to apprehend her. In Okmulgee, Chief of Police John Lung and Deputy Sheriff John Throckmorton gathered a posse of eight men and moved just before noon on June 6 to arrest Perryman.[35] The posse expected a pitched battle against "65 young Indians and negroes with her."[36] When the men arrived, they found that the crowd had dispersed, including Perryman.[37] She and Tulsay had moved to McAlester, Oklahoma, that morning.[38] The Creek Draft Rebellion ended with the only shots fired from the Henryetta Home Guard. The *Henryetta Free-Lance* declared that with the situation rectified, "it is not at all likely that there be any farther cause for investigation."[39] However, Jack Carter's syndicated news report began circulating, creating a grandiose Indian rebellion that never occurred.

The legacies of the Crazy Snake Uprising of 1909 and the Green Corn Rebellion in 1917 combined with the rumors about the June 5, 1918 meeting. Even if the draft did not play a large part in the discussions at the Stomping Grounds, the newspapers quickly made it the largest factor. Reporters pointed to pro-German influences on Ellen Perryman and the Creeks to explain their sudden rebellion. *The Sun*, of Pittsburg, Kansas, ran its headline as "Indians Rebel at Army Draft Under German Influence" and reported that Perryman herself was "in pay of the German government."[40] Other papers also included German influence in their articles and reported the various instances of disloyalty.

Several papers claimed that while in Washington, D.C., Ellen Perryman met with Phillip Enos, "a Philippino, who, officers here assert, is in the pay of the German government."[41] After this meeting, the *New York Times* claimed that she "has been lecturing among the tribes," telling the leaders that the government could not draft their men.[42] On top of this, the *Daily Oklahoman* reported that Perryman "is said to be attempting to organize a new secret society among the Indians, for the purpose of thwarting the government's plans to enlist Indians in war work."[43] However, confusion about the draft and the remote communities resulted in many difficulties that likely contributed to a lack of enrollment of Creek men. However, the papers used this fact as justification of their claims against Perryman.

Despite the reports, no evidence could be found to conclusively show Perryman's pro-German dealings or her anti-draft sentiments in June 1918. Regarding the questions of Creek loyalty, the Okmulgee County Council of Defense declared the news reports untrue regarding resistance to the draft. They released a statement saying a "competent investigation has revealed the story without foundation in fact."[44] Furthering the show of patriotism, "one hundred Creek Indians held an all-day loyalty meeting" at Hannah, Oklahoma, on June 14, 1918. The article pointed out that this meeting "sounds a great deal different from wild reports about Creek anti-draft uprisings."[45] The antiwar sentiment certainly fell among the minority of the Creek Nation. Many Creek men served, and some gave their lives in the United States military. The Creek Nation supported the United States in the war effort with supplies and manpower. Despite this, the sensational news reports about the dissension of the Creek Nation propelled them into the national spotlight.

Jack Carter had wired several newspapers that night, and once he returned to Henryetta, he called the various presses and told them his story. Carter's statement spread across the country and created the confusing stories and contradictory accounts. In fact, his story conflicted with the local newspaper reporters, who saw him as an ambitious correspondent who "copped out a few dimes and gave us some undesirable publicity."[46] His story "read like the old time Crazy Snake trouble" and inspired a chain of even more exaggerated sensational reports throughout the country.[47] Fortunately, local newspapers knew of his poor reputation as a reporter.

Jerry Rand, editor of the *Muskogee Phoenix*, revealed that he sent the bulletin to the Associated Press after receiving the information from Carter. Rand stated that he knew Carter "to be very unreliable in his manner of reporting news." To alleviate this, Rand toned down Carter's report before sending it to the Associated Press because he had lived in Oklahoma "long enough not to be misled by wild stories about Indian uprisings."[48] Unfortunately, since Carter sent the story to many different papers at once, others did not tone down Carter's exaggerated claims, creating the multitude of contradicting information. Due to this, Jerry Rand informed Jack Carter that they would no longer use his services for their paper. Furthering Carter's lack of honesty in his reports, H.B. Peairs, the superintendent of the Haskell Indian Institute in Kansas, believed that Carter's later affidavit detailing his interview with Ellen Perryman had been exaggerated. Peairs argued that Carter may have "felt that it was necessary to make a strong case against her because of his sensational newspaper reports."[49] Unfortunately, the shocking story had been released to the eager presses that expanded the stories to almost epic proportions.

The sensational headlines followed the story of Creek Indians arming themselves and moving on the warpath. To the white reporters, news of a Creek uprising meant bloodshed, and they reported to that extent without any confirmation. The largest exaggeration comes from the number of Creeks involved in the meeting at the Old Hickory Stomping Grounds. The report of Lieutenant Ray Wise stated that they found between twenty and thirty people assembled.[50] Other accounts put the number around fifty. Unfortunately, newspapers across the country exaggerated the numbers to give the sense of a large-scale uprising that would come with much violence. Many of the newspapers followed the *Daily Oklahoman* in reporting that two hundred Creeks went on the warpath.[51] The *El Paso Times* ran the headline "WHITES ARM AND PREPARE FOR BATTLE WITH REDMEN" and reported that the Henryetta Home Guards and one hundred civilians armed themselves to face five hundred "inflamed Creeks."[52] The most outrageous claim came from the *Norwich Bulletin* of Norwich, Connecticut, which reported that seven hundred Creek Indians "have armed themselves and taken refuge in the hills surrounding the Old Hickory stamping grounds."[53]

The articles that discussed the hundreds of armed Creeks also consistently declared that reports showed the group had killed three white farmers in the area. These reports show the societal fears and stereotypes regarding the Creek Nation. For example, the *Morning Tulsa Daily World* produced the standard report of two hundred hostiles and three dead farmers.[54] The news reporters thrived on stereotypical depictions of the Creek Indians. Stereotypes provide readers a "familiar foothold" to get them into a story.[55]

The sensationalism also transferred into the reasons for the rebellion. The fears of German intrusion in the affairs of Native Americans had played out in the media with the concern over dissent. Reporters also exaggerated the concerns into their stories. The *New York Times* blamed a "pro-German plot."[56] *The Sun* declared the Indians rebelled "under German influence."[57] The *Wilmington Morning Star* accused "German Propaganda."[58] No matter the cause, the reports all alluded to Ellen Perryman's alleged connection to German sympathizers in Washington, D.C. In their eyes, she had become public enemy number one because of her supposed attempts to turn the Creeks and other tribes against the United States government. However, these wild claims and stirring of public concern worried H.B. Peairs and Gabe Parker, superintendent for the Five Civilized Tribes.

While investigating the claims against Ellen Perryman and the Draft Rebellion, Peairs concluded that "the newspaper reports were found to be sensational." He made further inquiry into who originally reported the story, eventually finding Jack Carter. Peairs hoped that reports such as Carter's could be prevented in the future because of their inflammatory nature.[59] Parker believed the federal government should prevent sensational stories from being printed altogether. He argued that such stories, like those on the Creek rebellion, encouraged disloyalty and inspired resistance against the government. Parker thought the reports "are entirely pro-German in effect and ought to be classed with giving comfort, inspiration and aid to the enemies of our country."[60] Unbeknownst to Parker, the story printed in the *New York Times* did in fact inspire the German government.

During World War I, both sides created propaganda aimed at demoralizing the enemy. Demoralization of troops could change the course of a battle or even the war. To this effect, the Germans published a newsletter in English called *America in Europe: A Paper Published in the Interest of Good Fellowship Among*

All Nations and dropped it onto Allied troops. The propaganda would print stories attacking Allied government officials, news from Allied nations and articles discussing battles from their points of view. In the July 29, 1918 edition of the newsletter, the Germans published a small article on the Creek Draft Rebellion. It read, "The Creek Indians in Revolt: According to the *New York Times* the tribe of the Creek Indians refuse to allow their young men enter the United States Army. They are in open revolt. Three white men are reported to be killed in Oklahoma."[61]

While short, the article shows the damage Carter's sensational story had done. The misinformation may not have started as German propaganda, but it now served as such. The expansive coverage of the Creek Draft Rebellion as a German plot forced the Bureau of Indian Affairs to open an investigation.

On June 10, 1918, Commissioner Cato Sells instructed Gabe Parker to launch an investigation into the rebellion. The bad publicity tarnished the image of patriotic Native Americans that the Bureau of Indian Affairs had been cultivating throughout the war. Sells had been arguing for Indian participation in the war, stating, "If the native goes into this conflict as the equal and comrade of every man who assail autocracy and ancient might, he will come home with a new light in his face and a clearer conception of the democracy in which he may participate and prosper."[62] Any outburst against the government or war effort not only threatened to break the image Sells had created but also needed to be fully investigated and punished under the Sedition Act of 1918. Enacted on May 16, 1918, the act extended the Espionage Act of 1917 by outlawing more offenses, including speech against the government or the war effort. It banned the use of "disloyal, profane, scurrilous, or abusive language" regarding the United States government, its flag or its military. It also discouraged any talk that could cause others to view the American government with contempt.[63] Jack Carter's report accused Ellen Perryman of blatantly defying the act.

On June 11, Parker reported that his investigation found no disposition among the Creeks to resist the draft. He called Ellen Perryman "apparently demented" and claimed that her statements made to Jack Carter were "disconnected, visionary, and irresponsible."[64] This could have ended the matter, but the loyalty of the country's Native American inhabitants could not be taken for granted. Therefore, the Bureau of Indian Affairs could not sit idle when the people criticizing the government were their responsibility.[65] Parker's report began a nearly six-month-long investigation into the loyalty and actions of Ellen Perryman.

The policymakers in Washington ordered Parker to expand his search into Perryman's voiced opinions at the Stomping Grounds. Parker sent one of his field clerks, Harry B. Sedicum, to conduct a more thorough investigation. Sedicum conducted several interviews with eyewitnesses such as Lieutenant Ray Wise and Jack Carter. Sedicum went to the Old Hickory Stomping Grounds with Carter and others to investigate Perryman's statements. Upon arriving at the house of Jeff Francis, where Carter had spoken to Perryman the night of June 5, Carter questioned Francis. Carter claimed that on top of speaking against the government, Perryman possessed anti-government literature but did not let him see it. Francis claimed that Perryman did not make any speech to the gathered Creeks that night. On top of this, the Home Guard reports showed that the Creeks offered no armed resistance at all.[66] Sedicum's initial report seemed to find that none of the reports had any basis in fact. Despite this, Parker pushed Sedicum to dig deeper.

On June 17, Carl J. O'Hornett, a Henryetta realtor, backed Carter's story that Perryman made seditious statements in the presence of Jeff Francis, Jack Carter, Ben Turk and Ben Matthews. He called Perryman a "crazy person" and said that "something should be done with her."[67] As the story of the rebellion unfolded into a peaceful meeting gone awry by prejudiced white locals, Cato Sells asked Parker to investigate if the right to assemble had been infringed upon. Parker subsequently ordered Sedicum to interview several local Creeks to learn the facts about "the calling of the meeting, the purpose of the meeting, the number attending the meeting, the attitude of those in attendance, the subjects discussed by them, the attitude of visitors at the meeting, including representatives of the County Council of Defense, any county officers and any white people." Parker particularly wanted to know if white people attempted to break up the gathering and threatened the Indians to never meet again.[68] The concerns of the Creeks still needed to be protected if the investigation resulted in no evidence of sedition.

Ellen Perryman, in the meantime, began planning a new meeting at the Old Hickory Stomping Grounds to establish a Grand Army of the Republic post. In conversation with Gabe Parker, she appeared "incoherent and intensely prejudiced against people of the south." This odd dialogue prompted Parker to request Sells send an inspector for further investigation.[69] Sells sent H.B. Peairs to conduct the new investigation into Ellen Perryman. Peairs reported that the bureau had no occasion for alarm because the Creeks within the vicinity of the Stomping

Grounds were "quiet, peaceful, and…entirely loyal." He also remarked that he had yet to find any evidence confirming Perryman's disloyalty to the government.[70]

On June 22, 1918, Peairs acquired an affidavit from Jack Carter regarding the conversation he had with Ellen Perryman on June 5. Carter testified to Perryman's outrageous comments toward the government and her overall seditious attitude. This interview became the basis for the expansion of the investigation into Perryman. On August 8, 1918, W.L. Reed, an investigator working for James C. Davis, the national attorney of the Creek Nation, met with Perryman at Council Hill, Oklahoma.[71] When asked for a statement regarding Carter's testimony, Perryman refused, claiming that Carter led the mob that broke up their meeting on June 5. She also claimed that her trips to Washington were as an interpreter for other Indians working to get "the Loyal Creek Claim through Congress." Reed determined that Perryman "is undoubtedly demented, but I consider her perfectly harmless."[72]

Reed reported that Perryman believed that a price of $2,000 had been put on her head. She also stated that she could not take a drink of water in Henryetta because she feared being poisoned. She accused the Okmulgee County Council of Defense of poisoning all the wells and streams around the Old Hickory Stomping Grounds. Reed also stated that Perryman rambled in conversation, jumping quickly between topics. She concluded that she would not meet with James C. Davis unless she had a group of armed Indians to protect her from the mob she feared would attack her.[73]

Upon reading Reed's report, James Davis wrote to Gabe Parker that he believed Perryman to be a "rattle-brained, irresponsible person, given to constant talking." Although her conduct may have violated the Espionage Act, Reed did not suggest arresting her. He believed she did not have the mental capability to understand her actions, and if she were to be arrested, the Indians would resent this action and "it might lead to an uprising."[74] This new report helped H.B. Peairs conclude that the reports of Jack Carter "were overdrawn and painted in very glowing colors." Peairs believed that Perryman had made statements in her excitement that she would not have normally made. All evidence he had found proved her to be "a good citizen and a woman of good moral character and one who would not be guilty, under ordinary circumstances."[75] It seemed that the investigation against Ellen Perryman could be halted, as the reports all favored dropping the charges. Unfortunately, a new Creek uprising surfaced at the Hickory Stomping Grounds.

In early September, a rumor of another "Creek uprising" circulated around Oklahoma. Gabe Parker sent out men on September 7 to investigate these rumors before the meeting could happen. The investigators noted that they found no armed resistance, and the camped Creeks agreed to return home and register for the draft. In Henryetta, the team also found several white officers from Pontotoc and Hughes Counties present in Henryetta for the goal of squashing any resistance.[76] During this investigation, a Creek Indian gave authorities a translated letter from Ellen Perryman stating that "Indians are not citizens and do not have to register."[77] This letter, even though based in fact, convinced A. Bruce Bielaski, chief of the Justice Department's Bureau of Investigation, to issue a warrant for the arrest of Ellen Perryman.

A manhunt began as the Bureau of Indian Affairs attempted to capture Perryman. Many rumors circulated about her whereabouts, including one reported by H.A. Archer, a field clerk in Wewoka, Oklahoma. He reported that Perryman and a few other Creeks were in Washington, D.C., with "a representative of the German government" who promised the Indians immunity if they refrained from participating in the war; conversely, if they fought, they risked being treated harshly once Germany had won the war.[78] This report pushed Cato Sells to begin a local investigation in Washington. The new inquiry grew to involve the United States Post Office and the Secret Service. On October 18, 1918, Postmaster Willis W. Christopher in Kusa, Oklahoma, reported that Perryman and other Creeks had been corresponding with "some people at 468 Penna. Ave., N.W. Washington D.C."[79]

The hunt for Ellen Perryman continued until December 12, 1918, when authorities apprehended her in Oklahoma. Upon being arrested, she attacked the officers while "she pretended to be in a playful mood, but her blows were of the trip-hammer variety."[80] Perryman had her hearing for violating the Espionage Act on December 18 in Muskogee. However, since the war had ended on November 11, the court decided to postpone the case indefinitely and release Perryman on bond.[81] With this sentence, the story of the Creek Draft Rebellion ended. Despite finding no evidence of sedition on June 5, 1918, nor any sort of uprising, the Bureau of Indian Affairs had accused and hunted down Ellen Perryman just to release her.

The United States had found itself in an open conflict with the Creek Nation, but by the time the sensational news articles ran on June 6, the rebellion had begun and ended. The Creek Draft Rebellion existed only in the mind of prejudiced white locals and Jack Carter. A peaceful meeting to discuss tribal affairs encountered a conflict when attempting to buy flour. Carter's report sent the country into a hysteria over this Creek Draft Rebellion and vilified Perryman, which led to an investigation against her. The existence, or nonexistence, of the Creek Draft Rebellion is a culmination of public fears of dissension, exaggerated sensational reporting and the Bureau of Indian Affairs attempting to uphold the idea that all Native Americans supported the war effort. The arrest of Perryman ended the troubles of the Creek Draft Rebellion, but it became an inaccurate note in the history of Native American involvement in World War I.

Chapter 3

LIFE ON THE HOMEFRONT

During the war, the American public did not fully unite in support of the war in Europe. Dissent became a sign of weakness and support of the enemy throughout the country. To combat this and enforce national war policies, local patriots would use the Oklahoma State Council of Defense and its auxiliaries, the county councils of defense. Governor Robert L. Williams supported these local groups and declared it a patriotic duty. In a letter to important local leaders dated July 21, 1917, Governor Williams declared:

> *The emergencies of the war have made it necessary that both states and Nation take extraordinary steps in preparing the American people for their part in the world crisis. One of the chief organizations working to this end is the Council of National Defense, consisting of cabinet officers and an advisory commission, and under them, various state councils of defense.*
>
> *The problem confronting our own State Council of Defense is a big one. Before it lies the task of seeing that citizens of Oklahoma produce all of which they are possibly capable, that they care for themselves and also that they provide money and food and men for the needs of the Nation.*
>
> *The work of the State Council is effective only as it reaches the citizens, and the organization is now being extended with that aim in view. After a careful consideration of leading citizens, we are appointing you one of an executive committee of five, whose duty it shall be to organize a local County Council of Defense which shall work under the Oklahoma State Council and in other ways "coordinate the industries and resources of your county for the prosecution of the war."*

Service is without pay, a patriotic duty to your State and Nation in this time of great need for patriotism.[82]

Local citizens needed to give their undying support for the state to make sure that no rebellion, no slacking and no acts of dissent occurred in their districts.

The councils of defense held no actual legal power other than in the court of public opinion. To this, the state council told Hert in a letter dated August 1, 1917, "We wish to call to your attention the fact that your position has no legal status. Whatever authority you have is only that which the moral support of patriotic citizens of your community gives you."[83] However, the power of the councils of defense would quickly grow with the passing of the Espionage Act of 1917 and later the Sedition Act of 1918, which outlawed dissent and any speech that spoke ill of the government or military.

Suppressing dissent among American citizens became a driving factor in local patriotism. Newspapers and public speakers often spoke on the war and the requirement of every citizen to ensure victory overseas. The Oklahoma State Council of Defense created the Oklahoma Patriotic Speakers' Bureau, which gave speeches all over the state. The Four Minute Men, under the leadership of Glenn Condon, could give short speeches at a moment's notice to inspire patriotism. The council also created an Oklahoma Loyalty Bureau, which worked to locate and jail dissenters or any "slackers" who did not register for the draft. Loyalty cards were created and turned in to local councils of defense to provide a list of loyal Oklahomans.

The councils also focused on making sure that German communities did not harbor any anti-American feelings. Oklahoma, like many states, banned the speaking and teaching of the German language, which forced many German-language newspapers to cease. The constant harassment made many towns in Oklahoma change their names to remove their German heritage. For instance, Kiel became Loyal, Bismark became Wright and Korn became Corn.[84]

Perhaps the most significant legacy of the councils of defense came from the violence and public humiliation that many used to keep their communities free of dissent. Beatings, men being tarred and feathered, publicly painting men and businesses yellow, detectives investigating farmers and even murder came to define the tactics of the councils.

Perhaps the best example of the extremes of suppression is the murder of Joe Spring in Tulsa, Oklahoma, on March 23, 1918. L.S. Miller, who worked for the Tulsa County Council of Defense, shot Spring three times because he declared "that he hoped all American soldiers who went to France were killed." After surrendering himself to police, Miller was released, and his actions were declared justifiable homicide.[85]

In Payne County, the council of defense actively investigated its local farmers to ensure every acre of land was in use for the war effort. In April 1918, Hayden Land of Yale did not have eighty acres rented out for farming, so the council called on him to "rent it at once as it is time some crops were being put in."[86] On April 24, 1918, the council investigated a German immigrant, John Mandalier, who had lived in the United States for almost thirty years. He "refused to buy any Liberty Bonds or War Savings Stamps" and, when questioned, told the council he owed money to his siblings in Germany. The investigators recommended to the council, "Should you care to investigate further and get control of this money; I would advise you to take the matter up with the First National Bank of Ponca City as he does all his business through this bank."[87] Mandalier was brought before the council, and they determined that he should buy $100 of liberty bonds to show his patriotism to the United States, which he reluctantly did.[88]

All over the state, violence occurred as the vigilantism of the councils grew. The Choctaw County Council of Defense proudly recorded that "the application of a few courses of yellow paint, posting of slacker bulletins, and spankings administered with a heavy two-handed strap, have been found most expedient and efficacious remedies" in dealing with slackers and pro-Germans.[89] Once such instance from the Choctaw County Council of Defense was the public thrashing of Reverend Charles F. Reece. The council claimed to have letters in which he wrote derogatory remarks about the Red Cross. Therefore, they strapped him over a barrel and gave him one hundred lashes with a leather strap.[90]

In Braithwaite, John Aden, a local German businessman, was taken from his store by a masked mob and beaten. His troubles started with the council of defense after he spoke out against their attempt to stop the speaking of the German language. He also refused to buy liberty bonds and for this was removed from his position as postmaster.[91] In Norman, Oklahoma, a cage-like structure called the "slacker pen" was erected near the banks on Main Street. Citizens who came to town to deposit checks would be approached by men of the council, who would suggest how the money should go to various war organizations. If the citizen refused, they were placed inside the pen until they did what was asked of them.[92]

By the end of the war and thus the end of the reign of the councils of defense, the council boasted an impressive list of services that did not involve violence. The councils "contributed $149,250,000 to war funds." They created drastic sedition laws in many cities and towns making seditious statements an offense, took vigorous steps to provide for abundant harvest in 1918, furnished many comforts for the fighting men, stopped excessive profits and the hoarding of foods, standardized food prices, aided farmers to bring in feed stuff and seed from other states, kept coal mines working, led southern states in number of war gardens and issued 1,200,000 loyalty pledge cards.[93]

UNIVERSITY OF OKLAHOMA

For many citizens across the state, the need to participate in the war effort took precedence to show their loyalty. The councils of defense also extended their reach into the public universities of Oklahoma. The University of Oklahoma is a great example, as President Stratton Brooks served as secretary for the Oklahoma Council, Professor Chester Westfall was the director of wartime publicity and Professor Roy Gittinger also worked as the chair for the Cleveland County Council of Defense. Their connection perhaps added to the university's stance on the war effort.[94]

After the declaration of war, the university became inundated with patriotism. Students began to discuss dropping their studies to join the military. As a result, faculty met and declared that any student who left school to join in the war effort would receive full credit for their courses if they were passing when they left. Soon, many of the classrooms became emptier, and plays and shows were canceled without a full cast to perform.

On campus, President Brooks informed the male students that a volunteer regiment would be formed at the university so that the men could continue their studies while beginning a military regimen. Guy Williams, a veteran of the Mexican border crisis, was selected as the colonel. Attendance to the training would be compulsory, and all men were expected to do their part. In accordance with this, faculty immediately began acquiring equipment, uniforms, weapons and guides for the training of their students. Even the band participated by creating a thirty-piece regimental band for the unit. Sooner athletics also joined in, as Coach Bennie Owen became the lieutenant colonel for the regiment. He canceled practice to have the athletes train alongside the student soldiers.[95]

The female student body also did their part for the war effort by organizing a Red Cross society on campus that offered options for those who wanted to volunteer. They could choose one of three options, with Class A being willing to serve overseas, Class B serving anywhere in the United States and Class C serving at home. That day, 103 women signed up to volunteer. Shortly thereafter, a plan was organized to give a six-week course on Red Cross work at the university. It had around 160 women enrolled in April.[96]

As with the rest of the country, the war brought out many anti-German sentiments. As more and more opposition rose against those with German heritage, many citizens began to distance themselves from it. Professor Nathan Altshiller, for instance, decided to go into the Norman courthouse and have his name changed to Court, becoming Nathan A. Court.[97]

Faculty members also found ways to participate in the war effort beyond the council of defense or directly joining the military. Some professors, such as "historians E.E. Dale, James Buchanan, and Monroe Floyd, professors of law John Cheadle and Henry Foster, and Warren W. Phelan, director of the School of Education," gave patriotic lectures to soldiers at Camp Doniphan and Fort Sill. The university's extension service transformed into essentially a propaganda agency that provided patriotic speaking material to war speakers throughout the state. Other faculty found positions in the federal government or YMCA and saw service in Washington, D.C., or overseas.[98]

The University of Oklahoma's monumental shift to supporting the war effort soon found government support through the founding of the Student Army Training Corps (SATC). This would allow more men to stay in the United States to get an education in order to help rebuild Europe. However, it also served the dual purpose of training young men to eventually become officers in the United States Army. Many of the educated had come from the few military colleges around the country, such as West Point, Louisiana State University and Texas A&M, but the SATC would allow for officers from schools that did not have an established military education.[99]

All able-bodied male students had to enroll in the SATC, as the army appropriated buildings, equipment and dormitories from the university. Army officers came to the university to train the students and determine which candidates could be good officers. The University of Oklahoma received $900 for each student enrolled in SATC. This influx of cash became a lifeline to many struggling universities during the war. OU had around 1,173 students enrolled in SATC, which transformed the university into the appearance of a military camp with students wearing army uniforms, marching around campus and having drill, bayonet training and all the other features of military training.[100]

By the end of the war, the University of Oklahoma had been transformed into a well-oiled war machine. More than 2,300 students and faculty had contributed to the war effort, with 1,139 joining the service. As with many universities, many lives were lost in service to their country: 3 members of the faculty died, along with 21 students. The university fully organized to support the war effort, both abroad and at home, creating a legacy of service that continues to this day.[101]

CORDELL CHRISTIAN COLLEGE

Despite their success at the University of Oklahoma, the council of defense organizations did not always help the higher education institutions of the state. Their fanatical pursuit of those they considered disloyal or slacking in their patriotism knew no bounds, despite the complete lack of legal authority. In Washita County, in the town of Cordell, Oklahoma, the wrath of the local council of defense befell the Cordell Christian College, which led to the institution shutting its doors.

The college opened its doors in 1907 after being organized by J.C. Harrel, G.A.W. Fleming and W.D. Hockaday under the sponsorship of the Churches of Christ. The Churches of Christ took a pacifist approach to life, believing that killing, even in war, was wrong. They also believed that political systems were corrupt, so Christians should not vote. Instead, the members of the church sought to live quiet, pious lives.[102]

When the United States declared war on April 6, 1917, the college's beliefs came into conflict with the patriotic citizens of Oklahoma. To their credit, when Congress passed the draft, the college did send most of its male students to register. However, when President J.N. Armstrong and most of the faculty declared themselves to be conscientious objectors, many of the students followed suit. However, the local Cordell draft board refused to view the college as a theological school and, therefore, deemed that the students should not be allowed into noncombatant service. The draft board also worked to prevent the ministerial students from obtaining a ministerial exemption.[103]

Despite this early animosity, the college did support the war effort. The faculty and students frequently purchased liberty bonds and war savings stamps and followed the Food Administration guidelines like meatless days. Students assisted the Red Cross and worked in the neighboring fields picking cotton to assist in Oklahoma's agricultural increase to support the war. On top of this, thirty-eight students and three teachers had entered military service by July 1918. Unfortunately, to the people of Cordell, the pacifist sentiment at the college could not be overlooked.[104]

A few students ran afoul of the council of defense and local authorities, which only added to the negative perception of the college. Ben Randolph and Levi Wilment refused take a noncombatant status and were sent to prison at Fort Leavenworth. Leroy Epperson did not fill out his draft registration and was convicted as a deserter. Likewise, some of the faculty also drew punishment, such as W.D. Hockaday, who refused to buy liberty bonds. As a result, his store in Granite, Oklahoma, was painted yellow. His nephew Charles Clay also received a prison sentence at Fort Leavenworth after refusing to take noncombatant service. These instances began to cause the locals to accuse the school of being pro-German.[105]

In the May 16, 1918 edition of the *Gospel Herald*, Cordell Christian College's newspaper, a faculty member named S.A. Bell wrote an article discussing why it was wrong for Christians to support the military. The paper was sent to the local postmaster in Cordell, Henry Hubbard, who refused to mail the paper because the article was against the Sedition Act, which made any speech against the war illegal. Hubbard sent it up to the post office solicitor, W.H. Lamar, who agreed that the paper could not be distributed under the act. The post office then notified the Bureau of Investigation of this violation. Armstrong attempted to defuse the situation by publishing another article that decried the "radical statements" in Bell's article, but the damage had been done.[106]

On August 19, 1918, the Bureau of Investigation sent Special Agent J.G. Findley to investigate the college. The matter was short-lived, as Armstrong told Findley that the paper had ceased with the end of the school year, but the college continued to be under surveillance from the local council of defense and the bureau. The Washita County Council of Defense conducted its own investigation of Cordell Christian College. They interviewed several faculty members and discovered that not all members of the college supported Armstrong's ideals. With this, the council held a hearing on July 12 wherein they accused Armstrong and the college faculty of failing to support the war and discouraging young men from joining the war effort.[107]

During the hearing, the council discussed the multiple students who had been arrested for opposing military service and the lack of patriotic services. Unappeased with the answers Armstrong gave, another hearing pressed Hockaday about his failures to support the war effort and the actions of his nephew. In this line of questioning, Hockaday admitted that the school had taught "the doctrine of 'Absolutism' which opposed any military duty whatever." With this new "evidence," the Washita County Council of Defense issued an order to the college that the faculty must be reorganized to conform to military policies, all teachings must comply with military policy and Armstrong and allied faculty must be withdrawn from service at the college.[108]

The college resisted the pressure from the council and appealed to United States district attorney John Fain, who confirmed that the college had the legal protection to its views and doctrine. Therefore, the college appealed to the Oklahoma State Council of Defense, which ordered a hearing by Oklahoma State Supreme Court judge Thomas Owen. On August 13, Hockaday and Dial traveled to Cordell for the hearing. Hockaday met with Alvin Bingaman, the chairman for the county's council of defense. Their conversation became heated, and Bingaman threatened that the citizens would close down the school regardless of the hearing's decision. Threats of mob violence quickly arose until the timely arrival of Jude Owen, who calmed the tension for the moment.[109]

In the hearing, Bingaman failed to present any substantial evidence to show that Armstrong or the college had violated the law. Judge Owen declared that the faculty and college were free to continue their work unopposed. While this decision exonerated the college, it did not mean that the local council or Bingaman agreed. Instead, the council of defense increased their harassment of Armstrong and the college, asking for more investigations into both. The threats from the council also became more violent, which led to the board of regents deciding to have Armstrong resign as president and disband the school. Thus, the Cordell Christian College ceased to exist due to an overzealous council of defense.[110]

LIBERTY LOANS

With the outbreak of the war, the United States found itself woefully unprepared for a large-scale war in Europe. It had no army, navy or transports that could compete with the Central Powers. Therefore, the United States Congress authorized the sale of $5 billion in bonds to quickly raise the money needed to support our allies and our own mobilization. Oklahoma received a quota to sell $14.5 million worth of bonds. To accomplish the oversight for this large initiative, the council of defense took charge of the drives to raise money. The fear of having their loyalty questioned drove many county councilmen to extremes to raise their quota.[111]

To assist in the process, the Oklahoma state council published the *Liberty Loan Handbook*, which outlined the entire process. Councils should set up patriotic gatherings with speeches from prominent citizens or the Four Minute Men to inspire patriotism and the giving of funds for the war effort. Bonds could be purchased for as low as twenty dollars with a return of 3.5 percent interest a year. Many Oklahoma banks adopted the idea that "it is the patriotic duty of every citizen to by as many liberty bonds as possible."[112]

The council officials quickly realized that pools of money residing in Native communities could easily be used for the war effort through the white "guardians of Native children. For instance, Probate Judge H.L. Staudervan ruled that J.D. Porter, the guardian of a wealthy Native minor could invest $25,000 of the boy's money in bonds. Likewise, in Muskogee, Judge Enloe V. Vernon forced the purchase of $25,000 in bonds upon the guardians of Edith Durant, a young Creek girl."[113]

As the First Liberty Loan drive ended in June 1917, the Oklahoma City Chamber of Commerce took an example from the council of defense and appointed a "strong arm" committee with the goal of tracking down any and all slackers. The committee would gather anyone they saw as slacking in their giving to the liberty bonds and publicly embarrass them and give them "a chance to buy bonds or show valid reason for not buying them." To avoid this fate, business firms or individuals targeted by the committee would have to purchase a predetermined amount of bonds.[114] At the end of the first drive in June, fear and patriotism had become the driving factors of a successful fundraiser.

To this point, on June 14, 1917, the *Daily Oklahoman* told readers, "Buy a bond and proclaim yourself a patriot—not a traitor." The article stated, "You have to take your stand, with America, or against her." Citizens would have to purchase a liberty bond to prove their loyalty or face the consequences. The article also warned that the Oklahoma City Chamber of Commerce would be creating a list of those who had bought bonds to determine those who did not. This position would force Oklahoma businesses to give more in the next bond drive.[115]

In October 1917, the Second Liberty Loan drive began with a quota of $30 million for Oklahoma. Once again, state officials wanted to volunteer money from Native Americans to bolster the bond drive. Gabe Parker, the Oklahoma superintendent of the Five Civilized Tribes, recommended that $2 million in Native money be invested, which was authorized by the commissioner of Indian Affairs. In Muskogee, Oklahoma, the courts brought seventy-five guardians of Native wards to find out why their money had not been invested in bonds and encourage them to give freely.[116]

The drive would be finished by the end of October. This short timeframe made the council of defense and chamber of commerce even more zealous in their attempt to root out slackers. The chamber threated to publicly read the names of wealthy citizens who had not given to the drive. This indeed enticed many wealthy men to purchase bonds, but it was not enough. The chamber beefed up its "strong arm" committee with a second slacker wagon to round up anyone they believed to be lax in their donation. In the end, the state fell almost $4 million short. Fortunately, American troops had finally begun to enter combat overseas by the end of the year, which put some relief on the extreme patriotism as the reality of losing a large part of the workforce started to affect the state.[117]

Chapter 4

NATIVE AMERICAN PARTICIPATION

Native Americans played a large role in World War I, with more than twelve thousand serving in the military. By percentage, Native American communities gave more men and had more casualties than white solders. In fact, almost 50 percent of eligible Cherokee men served in the military.[118] The various tribes participated in the war effort both abroad and at home through service and supporting the war effort. Many tribal members joined the war due to in part to the high levels of acculturation within the United States. Still others joined to escape their small communities, seek out the traditional path of combat, show pride as Americans or just defend their country. No matter their reasoning, service in the war increased feelings of patriotism and a feeling of being American throughout Native American communities, which would eventually lead to citizenship for all Natives.

World War I was not the first time Native Americans had fought for the United States. Native troops had been employed since the first European settlers landed in North America. In March 1916, many Native men joined the Oklahoma National Guard to participate in defending the southern border. When the United States declared war on Germany, military leaders hoped that Native Americans could be counted on to be a fierce fighting force. After all, the United States military had spent the last fifty years combating Native tribes throughout the West. The implementation of Native troops became a hotly debated topic, as some people such as Joseph Dixon, a photographer and staunch supporter of Native citizenship, argued for segregated Native regiments like the British used with colonial troops. Ultimately, Native Americans served alongside white soldiers in integrated units. Government officials hoped that military service would help to "Americanize" Native Americans by forcing them to learn English and skills they could use to assimilate into the American culture and prove their loyalty to the United States.[119]

The Selective Service Act of 1917 created a draft that required all men between the ages of twenty-one and thirty-two to register. This created an interesting problem with Native Americans, as many tribes did not have American citizenship. Therefore, they were technically exempt from the draft, but many registered regardless and would serve when called on. Between the draft and regular enlistment, around 25 percent of the adult male Native population served in the military.[120] On top of this, the other 75 percent were encouraged to join the war effort via the Food Administration. The Bureau of Indian Affairs believed that more than thirty thousand Native Americans in Oklahoma could work to support the agricultural demand of the war. An emphasis on wheat, beans, corn and potatoes helped get the rural communities involved in their patriotic duties. The government even printed pamphlets in the Cherokee language.[121]

The war effort also aided in relations between certain tribal entities and the American government. For instance, the Nighthawk Keetoowahs had protested the Dawes Allotment Act of 1887 and established a movement of returning to traditional Cherokee ways of life. However, the war allowed for a meeting of Bureau of Indian Affairs superintendent Gabe Parker and the leader of the Nighthawks, Red Bird Smith. The result was a new spirit of cooperation, as the Nighthawks agreed to cultivate dozens of acres of corn for the war effort.[122] This band was not alone, as Chickasaws, Creeks, Seminoles, Kiowas and Choctaws cultivated crops at "unprecedented levels."[123]

In military service, Native men served throughout the army and navy, with the highest percentages serving in the 36th Division (Oklahoma-Texas National Guard) and the 90th Division (Oklahoma-Texas Draftees). The 36th Division would boast around one thousand Native soldiers. Nineteen of these soldiers from the Choctaw Nation pioneered the practice of using Native American languages as military code for communications. The Choctaw Code Talkers of the 142nd Infantry Regiment would be credited with the success of a withdrawal from Chufilly, as their communications could not be deciphered by the Germans. In these roles, many Native men would go on to achieve military glory in combat and secure a legacy for Native soldiers.

The concept of Natives as a warrior society meant that many of the white officers would assign them scout duties on the front lines, which led to a mortality rate five times that of their white counterparts.[124] This same conception also translated into German perspectives of Native American soldiers. The German people were obsessed with Native Americans, thanks to German author Karl May, who became one of the most celebrated German writers of all time. His stories revolved around a fictional Native American hero named Winnetou and his adventures in the American West. The ferocity of Native fighters terrified the German soldiers when they learned that the Canadians and Americans employed Native American soldiers. For the Germans, the fear of being scalped would cause many to surrender or specifically target Native troops.[125]

Charles Robert Ward of Nowata, Oklahoma, served in Company K, 358th Infantry, 90th Division, going overseas on June 20, 1918. He participated in the St. Mihiel and Meuse-Argonne Offensives. In the Argonne, he earned a Distinguished Service Cross for eliminating several German snipers. He recalled:

> *I was out after snipers. I just got out on the fill. I was lying on the ground. They told me that there were four snipers who were playing havoc with our machine guns and that they must be brought down. And I was detailed to bring them down, and I had not more than stretched myself on the ground before the sniper got after me. A bullet struck my helmet on the ground and went out the back, ripped the back of my coat clear down. I had shot one sniper at my left. And then it happened that the other snipers fired and struck the side of the helmet, and it went clear through and beyond me. I thought it was time for me to be getting out of there, and as quickly as possible I brought down both of those snipers and then the third one, and was off, and for this I received my distinguished service medal.[126]*

Thomas Muskrat of Webbers Falls, Oklahoma, originally went overseas with Company F, 165th Infantry, 36th Division, but at some point transferred to Company F, 165th Infantry, 42nd Division. He enjoyed his time on the automatic rifle squad, recalling, "I loved to load up and then let drive on the Boche. There is so much that I can't put it into English. Big shells dropping all around us. Didn't excite me. I wanted to pick them up and hurl them back in their faces."[127]

Sam Beaver of Lyons, Oklahoma, belonged to the Creek and Cherokee Nations. He originally went overseas with Company F, 144th Infantry, 36th

Tsianina Redfeather. *Signal Corps Photograph.*

Division, but transferred to Company B, 23rd Infantry, 2nd Division, in France. On November 1, 1918, Beaver was killed in action during an attack on enemy-held positions just outside the German-occupied French town of Landres-et-Saint-Georges, France, during the Meuse-Argonne Offensive.

JOSEPH OKLAHOMBI of McCurtain County, Oklahoma, served in Company D, 141st Infantry, 36th Division. He participated in the St. Mihiel and Meuse-Argonne Offensives. On October 8, 1918, while fighting around St. Etienne, Oklahombi and 23 soldiers attacked an enemy position and captured 171 prisoners. They then held their position for several days against brutal counterattacks. For this, Oklahombi received the Silver Star and Croix de Guerre.

TSIANINA REDFEATHER of Eufaula, Oklahoma, belonged to the Muscogee (Creek) Nation. Before the war, she had a successful career in vaudeville. During World War I, she traveled overseas with a group of Native performers and performed a show titled *The Indian of Yesterday and Today* to American soldiers. They showcased customs and dances of their tribes, which provided many soldiers their first look at Native culture.[128]

The actions of Oklahoma's Native American population as well as those in the rest of the country did not go unnoticed by the government. After the war, reports of Native heroism frequently appeared in the newspapers, and talks of recognition by the country they served became a hot topic. This culminated in all Native Americans receiving American citizenship in 1924.[129]

Chapter 5

FLU EPIDEMIC

Between September 1918 and April 1919, approximately 7,500 Oklahomans died from the influenza virus and the pneumonia that followed. Another 93,000 people fell sick but recovered from the terrible virus.[130] Worldwide, influenza may have killed over 50 million people, some 670,000 of those being American. The 1918 influenza outbreak is commonly referred to as the Spanish flu, though the epidemic likely began in the United States at Camp Funston, Kansas. In March 1918, over 1,000 soldiers fell ill, with 38 dying of complications. From here, the disease likely spread along with the troops as they moved around the country in preparation for their service in Europe.

In the fall of 1918, the virus expanded to become one of the deadliest viral outbreaks in recent history. October was the initial outbreak that brought the United States and Oklahoma to a standstill. In Oklahoma, some 1,249 cases were reported throughout twenty-four counties. Pneumonia was the main cause of death, but it and influenza are so closely linked that even today, modern international health statistics routinely classify them as a single cause of death. Influenza causes pneumonia either directly, by a massive viral invasion of the lungs, or indirectly, by destroying parts of the body's defenses and allowing bacteria to infect the lungs. Despite the high death toll, most victims recovered. In the United States, the virus led to pneumonia in only 10 to 20 percent of all cases. However, those few were most likely to be fatal.[131]

This strand of influenza targeted the young and healthy, those who traditionally do not die from influenza. Those who contracted pneumonia were subject to terrible suffering. The body developed mahogany spots over the cheekbones, and soon after the cyanosis began to extend from their ears and spread all over their face. Cyanosis occurs when victims start to turn blue because their lungs can no longer transfer oxygen into their blood. The lips, ears, nose, cheeks, tongue, fingers and sometimes the entire body could take the appearance of a dusky, leaden blue. The victims continually coughed up blood while it also poured out of mucus membranes, namely the nose, ears, eye sockets and vagina. The lungs filled with a frothy, bloody fluid that caused rupturing. These ruptures could cause pockets of air to leak out just under the skin, causing air pockets called subcutaneous emphysema. A navy nurse noted that these pockets made patients crackle like rice crispies when they were rolled onto their sides. Some victims also suffered lost vision and paralysis of ocular muscles. Finally, the disease ravaged internal organs. It caused blood to flood the brain and damage to the kidneys, and the muscles of the rib cage were torn apart by the external stress of heavy coughing.[132]

OKLAHOMA CITY

On September 16, 1918, an Oklahoma City doctor reported that he had treated a patient with a "heavy cold" but would not call it the flu. However, over the next couple of weeks, more and more patients appeared with similar symptoms. City and health officials refused to accept that the Spanish influenza had reached Oklahoma City and believed they could control the outbreak. Over the next month, the flu would quickly spread throughout the state, killing thousands.

By October 1, over five thousand people had flooded the city hospitals, filling up all beds and spilling into the hallways. Nurses and doctors also fell victim to the virus, reducing the hospitals' ability to treat the ever-increasing number of patients. Doctors could not agree on a treatment plan for patients, and the quickness of death meant that bodies were constantly being carted out of the hospital and piled up.

Life in the city came to a screeching halt. Travel ceased, as hotels could not keep staff due to sickness. For instance, the Lee-Huckins Hotel reported that half of the staff had contracted the flu. Not too long after, the conductors of the Oklahoma Railway, who ran the streetcar so important to early urban travel, fell ill and could not operate their vehicles. The economy and everyday logistics of life soon failed: supply lines halted as truck drivers fell ill; employees of drugstores could not distribute medicine without staff or supplies; mail could not be delivered without carriers; phone calls could not be made without operators.[133] On top of this, government officials soon took ill, meaning a halt to any decision-making that could help alleviate the situation. "With city government decapitated, hospitals filled to capacity, doctors and nurses working 48-hour shifts, communication and transportation systems on life support and the working life in the city a shambles, it was shaping up to be one of the most dire periods in Oklahoma City's history."[134]

To aid the struggling healthcare system, the Red Cross mobilized for assistance. Women were recruited to serve as nurses and do their part for the war effort. Their enemy was influenza. Rather than focusing on the hospitals, the Red Cross worked to find those ill who could not get to a hospital. The families trapped in their homes without the means for transportation needed to be cared for. Women went door to door looking for sick people and cared for them. They would bring food, clean the home, help with laundry and then move on to the next house. Meanwhile, other Red Cross volunteers tirelessly sewed flu masks, pneumonia jackets and outfits for flu victims.

Seeing the severity of the outbreak, Oklahoma City quickly placed the city under a quarantine. All public places such as schools, theaters and even churches were closed. Children were not allowed to be out in the city in groups, spitting was outlawed and the police broke up any gathering they came across. This proved difficult to enforce, as the police department had also been hit hard by the flu and had only a few officers fit for service in the city. Fortunately, the closing of the schools meant that nearly fourteen thousand children had been freed up to enter the workforce in different capacities. Children helped their family stores, worked with the Red Cross to care for the sick or acted as carriers and operators for communications.

Throughout October, the number of deaths continued to rise. The Red Cross frequently found heartbreaking scenes of families who had come down with the flu and, without access to hospitals, lost the children, the parents or both. Alberta F. Daugherty, who had become one of the most influential and leading figures in the Red Cross in Oklahoma City, recalled many instances of devastated families. In one case, a young mother was so sick that she could not nurse or feed her weeks-old infant. The baby died, but the mother did not even have the strength to close the baby's eyes. When Red Cross workers found her, they reported she suffered mentally from staring into her dead child's eyes for several days.[135]

Daugherty fought tirelessly to make sure that the poor and working class of the city had medical attention. Hospitals in the city were filled to capacity already and refused to take in new patients, especially those who could not pay. Daugherty publicly called for city officials to open new emergency hospitals and fund the care of the city's poor. Exhausted and infuriated, Daugherty appealed to Oklahoma City commissioner of public safety Mark Kesler, but he had left the city to visit his mother in Kansas City. Daugherty then aired her frustrations to anyone who would listen, which angered Kesler. He reportedly phoned Daugherty and berated her for her actions and "playing politics."[136]

This upset a local attorney and chair of the Red Cross Committee, David I. Johnston, who then led a group of angry citizens into the mayor's office and demanded Kesler resign. On October 17, the sick mayor Ed Overholser and City Commissioner Jack Walton attended a meeting with Dr. George Hunter, the city physician; Commissioner Mike Donnelly; the city finance chief, David Johnston; Mark Kesler; and Alberta Daugherty. Immediately, the group demanded that Kesler resign for his lack of actions to combat the outbreak and his attack on Daugherty's character. Johnston and Daugherty plainly placed the situation before the group of the city's failure to support the poor families in their community and demanded that the emergency hospitals be opened and the city accept responsibility for *all* of its citizens. Seeing the writing on the wall, both Kesler and Hunter tendered their resignations. Control of the city's health facilities was turned over to the Red Cross, and the city offered all the financial assistance it could give.

The Red Cross immediately got to work. The plan called for breaking the influenza problem into three categories. The first two focused on the patients by putting them into two types: those who needed immediate admission to a hospital and those who were recovering but needed food and medicines. Finally, the entire city would need to be scrubbed to avoid the spread of other diseases such as cholera or tuberculosis.

To accomplish this task, the Red Cross sent volunteers to every household in the city to find flu victims. Those who could not or would not leave their homes were forced out by police and taken to hospitals. Unsurprisingly, Packingtown, one of the poorest areas of the city, composed mostly of immigrants, had been hit the hardest. Every house had at least one case present. To provide adequate care, emergency hospitals were opened in the First Presbyterian Church, Oklahoma City Country Club and the community center. In addition, the Liberty Kitchen, which had been providing food for troops traveling through the city, switched over to feeling flu patients at the city's expense.

Finally, the city's Public Works Department rounded up as many men as it could find to scrub down the entire city. They picked up trash from every inch of the city and scrubbed the streets and buildings with soap and water. Boardinghouses were inspected and either cleaned up or condemned to avoid any further contamination.

These policies and work finally helped to turn the fight against the flu by the end of the month. The number of new cases began to drop significantly, and more people were released from the hospitals. The outbreak appeared to be under control, but the city would not lift its quarantine or bans on public gatherings. It took until November 9 for the city to lift its bans on gatherings. People flocked to the theaters or into the public squares to rejoice. Two days later, the announcement of the armistice that ended hostilities in Europe brought out the community in droves to celebrate the end of the war and the end of their nightmare at home.[137]

BARTLESVILLE, OKLAHOMA

The war effort brought great wealth to the area, as Bartlesville soon became the top provider of lead and zinc to the war effort. This huge boom brought even more prosperity and growth to the city. Unfortunately, this meant that the city needed to expand in order to adjust to the great smelter industry.[138] Between 1910 and 1920, the census records show that Bartlesville expanded from a population of 6,181 to 14,417.[139] The land easiest to expand to was west into the smelter communities, especially Smeltertown, as the streets, sewers and water had already been improved to meet the city standards. The only problem with this was the Polish communities already settled on the land.

In Bartlesville, Frank M. Overlees and his brother Jess had entered the real estate business early in the city's founding. They had secured land and sold it to the city in additions.[140] The Second Overlees Addition was opened in 1907 as the Polish immigrants moved into the area, and some of the land was settled by them, thus forming part of Smeltertown. By 1917, the lots of the Third Overlees Addition, which encompassed even more parts of Smeltertown, had come up for sale. The Overlees family advertised the land as exceedingly attractive to those desirous of owning their own home. They promoted the sale by stating that the area had been updated with drainage and "while outside the city will have water and gas, and without city taxes."[141] With some of the land in both additions settled by Polish immigrants, the city and the Overlees family needed to find ways to remove them to expand their own interests.

However, World War I brought most of the city growth programs to a halt as men joined or were drafted into the military. The city of Bartlesville and the smelter communities kept producing the much-needed lead for the war effort and paused their expansions. In the fall of 1918, the war had almost reached its end. Despite the high death toll of the war, the world suffered another catastrophic attack, this one biological. In September, the influenza epidemic hit Oklahoma. This epidemic was caused by the flu that followed with pneumonia. In the United States, estimates suggest 28 percent of the country became infected and at least 670,000 died. In Oklahoma, the disease swept through the state from mid-September 1918 to April 1919, killing an estimated 7,350.[142] Bartlesville suffered greatly during the epidemic, having one of the highest ratios of flu deaths to population in the country.[143] The city attempted to combat the spread of influenza by pulling the community together for support, but they also took the opportunity to push out the immigrant Polish communities.

The first cases of influenza struck Oklahoma City on September 29, 1918.[144] To prepare Bartlesville for the epidemic, Lyda W. Anderson, director of nursing services of the Southwest Division Red Cross, called for aid in meeting the local demand that might arise. She called for the local group to "register and prepare for mobilization all of the available nursing resources of your community with as little delay as possible…in the event of visitation of this epidemic."[145]

On October 5, 1918, the *Morning Examiner* published the first reported death from influenza in the community: Lloyd Pope.[146] That same day, a train arrived in Bartlesville as part of a Liberty Loan campaign to garner support and get people to save their fruit pits and nutshells for gas masks. A special car on the train featured captured German war trophies such as weapons, artillery, helmets and so on. This spectacle drew "an immense crowd" to Union Station, which likely led to a quick dissemination of influenza.[147] Only four days after the train arrived, the City of Bartlesville ordered all city schools, pool halls, movie theaters and churches to close until the end of the week. Nearly four hundred reported cases of influenza and several deaths caused the county to issue emergency procedures. The newspapers published a list of precautions to take against the flu, including avoiding crowds, bundling in clothing, keeping bedroom windows open and drinking plenty of water.[148]

The city began attempts to control the spread of disease by closing all public buildings and urged parents to keep their children indoors. To protect the children, the city announced a strictly enforced anti-spitting ordinance during the epidemic. Anyone caught spitting on the sidewalk or in any public building faced immediate arrest.[149] This idea of protecting children by closing public spaces eventually led to a new problem of "too many youngsters downtown." To solve this, Bartlesville leaders declared that if it continued, the children would be picked up by police.[150]

As the flu ravaged Bartlesville, the city continued to educate the populace to slow the spread of sickness. The city board of health worked with the influenza committee of the Red Cross to open a temporary bureau of information. The bureau kept a daily record of all new cases, explained preventive treatments and provided bulletins of information. They also kept a list of nurses and helpers available and assisted in placing these volunteers in homes where members were afflicted with the flu. Finally, the bureau provided, free of charge, pneumonia jackets to warm the chests of sufferers, as well as contagion masks, both made by the women's work department of the Red Cross.[151]

By October 12, 1918, the high number of cases had left every available clinic and physician struggling to keep up. Attempting to alleviate the situation, the local Elks Lodge opened its third floor to the community to be used as an emergency flu hospital.[152] The temporary accommodation received fifty cots from the Empire Company and two nurses, one to work during the day and the other at night. The committee in charge of this hospital asked that those who could pay for their care do so, but those unable would be cared for at no cost. They hoped that the temporary help would solve the problem for many people who lived outside the city in the smelter communities. The hospital called for volunteers to donate sheets and their time to cook for the sick and nurses as one of their patriotic duties.[153]

By October 12–14, the area saw 122 new cases, with 8 deaths reported in only two days. The Elks Lodge hospital had 19 cases under its care. But the city officials noticed that the west side of Bartlesville in Smeltertown had the highest portion of cases and deaths. The deplorable sanitary conditions of this part of town drew criticism, as "victims lie on floors without mattresses or bed coverings."[154] Doctors who entered that part of the city were called into almost every home to check on someone stricken with the disease. Some homes had every member of the family down with influenza. The Influenza Committee saw this and called for any women to volunteer to aid in the crisis. The women were asked to go into some of the homes where all the members were ill and prepare their meals and do other work to relieve their distress. The mortuary section of the same newspaper furthered their plight, with 10 reported deaths from influenza/pneumonia; 7 of them were residents of Smeltertown. In a sad hand of fate, 3 of them were brothers, one of whom died of influenza in an army camp the same day.[155]

The high number of victims in the smelter communities had a variety of factors. The poor sanitation of the area without proper sewage or water systems aided in the weakened immune systems of residents. Some citizens of Bartlesville blamed the pollution of the air from the sulphuric fumes of the smelters.[156] Stanley Kazmierzak, who grew up in the area, blamed the strain that the heat and arduous work took on the workers for their compromised immune systems. Kazmierzak volunteered at one of the hospitals during the epidemic and recalled that if patients had pneumonia, they would pass away. He remembered the terrifying efficiency with which death struck those afflicted: "I wheeled them in from ambulances and put the sheet over them, and I wheeled them out the back door."[157]

In response to the claims of Smeltertown being the center of the influenza outbreak, Mayor Easter and the city sanitary officer, Bud Phillips, toured the west side of the city to answer complaints that numerous homes were surrounded by unsanitary conditions. The area toured happened to be that within and immediately adjacent to the Third Overlees Addition that the city was interested in acquiring. The mayor found a number of filthy pig sties and unsanitary outhouses, but when he confronted the immigrant owners about how they would fix the problems, they responded by claiming that since they were outside city limits, he had no authority to order them around. The mayor then threatened, "Leave it alone and you will find yourself in police court Monday night." He declared he would arrest the tenants and owners if the place was not cleaned up.[158]

Unfortunately for the residents of both communities, flu victims continued to fill the Elks Lodge emergency hospital. The facility was understaffed, and the tedious work quickly drained the women running the place. This sudden rush pushed the emergency accommodations past its limits. The facilities became so crowded that they accepted the offer of the Baptist church to open its two large classrooms for patients. This second emergency hospital provided another fifty cots for influenza patients. Dr. Mary Barns took control of the facility and designated two small rooms to be used for dangerous cases. To accommodate this expansion, the YMCA offered its basement for storage of all supplies of both facilities. The Red Cross canteen committee opened a kitchen in the local Methodist church to provide meals for the nurses and patients in the two emergency hospitals.[159]

The Baptist hospital quickly started to fill its empty cots. By October 17, it had 32 patients, while the Elks Lodge had 27. Ambulances, their drivers and attendants wearing gauze masks kept busy by traveling to Smeltertown, where the disease continued to rage virulently. This large influx of patients forced the Baptist church to open an additional room in the basement. The wards soon filled.[160] The kitchen in the Methodist church, on top of supplying the two emergency hospitals, began serving food to the families of Smeltertown, helping almost 280 people.[161]

Despite Bartlesville's aid to the smelter communities, the *Washington County Sentinel and the Weekly Enterprise* declared in an article that it was time to act against Smeltertown. The article argued that the fatality of the influenza had been noted in Smeltertown because the sanitary conditions made it impossible to combat the disease. Therefore, the City of Bartlesville should take over the area. It continued by declaring Smeltertown as a city within itself yet without the ordinary sanitary equipment such as sewers, ordinances, health precautions, police protection or fire protection. In many instances, nurses claimed to have found sanitary conditions most deplorable without any city law to intervene.[162] The city would take action because "there is no way to force them to clean up their premises because they are without the jurisdiction of the city yet they are contingent of the city and their fetid breath contaminates the families who are near them and who desire to live under sanitary conditions."[163]

This blame of Smeltertown as the center of the epidemic continued in the press. On October 18, the *Morning Examiner* stated that the "area of infection spreads to North Bottoms from Smeltertown where it had previously centered." That day, many of the cases in the hospitals came from the North Bottoms, whereas previously "practically all" cases had come from Smeltertown. Physicians declared that if a cool, hard rain would come to Smeltertown, it would do much to stop the spread of the disease, as it would settle the germ-laden dust and clear the atmosphere. In conjunction, the Bartlesville Interurban Railway Company closed its cars from Dewey to Smeltertown after 8:00 p.m. every day due to the extreme shortage of labor and decrease in riders.[164]

On October 19, almost a week after the mayor's threats to Smeltertown, the police moved into the area to force the cleanup of the pig sties within the Overlees Addition. The officers moved through the districts outside the city limits and ordered the people who maintained the pigs to move them out into the country. Some of the owners argued that they were not subject to city regulations, but the officers enforced the order of the city health authorities by claiming their scope of influence extended beyond the immediate city limits. The other citizens of the area claimed to be exerting their combined effort to have the pig sties, and by extension their owners, permanently removed.[165]

The next day, the city announced that it would open another emergency hospital at the Presbyterian church to care for the numerous infants of stricken parents.[166] Fortunately for the city, the influenza epidemic began to recede by October 20. The news reported fewer deaths and more cured patients from the hospitals every day. It also finally referred to the Mexican and Black population of the smelter communities who had not been given access to the main hospitals. On October 29, Dr. Powell, a Black physician, was credited for doing his bit during the epidemic by attending "seven Mexicans, twenty-two negroes, and ten whites."[167]

Despite the recession of the pandemic, the city continued its campaign to clean up the area of Smeltertown in the Overlees Addition. On October 22, the "big offensive" continued to rid the area of pig sties. The *Morning Examiner* revealed the location of the pigs and that the reason was for the stench, not sanitation.

> In one block in the Overlees Addition it is reported that there were no less than twenty-nine pigs being kept by residents of that section. The stench from these pens has become unbearable to other neighbors and they complained so vigorously that County Health Officer C.E. Weber and City Health Officer Woodring ordered them to be cleaned up at once.

This cleaning meant removal from the area, as Deputy Sheriff Creed served notice on every tenant to move the pens.[168]

That same day, a man was seen scattering a white powder from a motor car on the west side of the city. The situation was reported, and a sample was taken to a chemist for analysis.[169] The next day, the city revealed that the powder scattered around the smelters was a disinfectant for the purpose of safeguarding the health of the people residing in that part of town.[170] That same day, the City of Bartlesville increased its crusade to clean up the Overlees Addition.

A squad of twenty men of Company E of the Oklahoma National Guard under command of Sergeants East and Fisher was called in to force the cleanup of Smeltertown. The *Morning Examiner* claimed that the guardsmen would remain until the filthy conditions in certain neighborhoods were remedied. The owners of pigs in the Overlees Addition had sold their pigs and had them shipped out of town in response to the demand and pressure from the city and county health authorities. However, the newspaper reiterated that this removal was not a sanitation issue for the health of the residents but rather because the foul-smelling pens had been a nuisance to their neighbors.[171]

By November, the influenza epidemic had cleared up enough to discharge all the babies from the Presbyterian hospital as more patients were released from the emergency facilities. The schools, churches and other public spaces opened once more, and life began to return to normal. Unfortunately, the epidemic took a heavy toll on Bartlesville and the smelter communities. An exact number is not known, but the city suffered hundreds of deaths because of the outbreak. At one point, Bartlesville had the second-highest ratio of flu deaths to population in the nation, trailing only Philadelphia.[172] The smelter workers suffered a sizable portion of the deaths. In one week during the pandemic, forty residents of Frog Hollow died at a time when there were only thirty homes in the neighborhood.[173]

World War I essentially ended with the armistice signed on November 11, 1918, ending all armed hostilities. With the end of hostilities, the demand for lead and zinc fell dramatically, causing the smelter workers to lose work. On top of this lack of work, the City of Bartlesville finally made its move by annexing parts of Smeltertown. On December 3, 1918, the city took in the Second Overlees Addition by action of the city commissioners.[174] The city planned to extend the sewer system, paved roads and waterworks into the area now that it was officially part of the city. On January 6, 1919, Bartlesville annexed the Third Overlees Addition, where they had previously forced out the pig sties and their owners. The city accomplished this by declaring an emergency "for the preservation of the public peace, health, and safety." Thus, the annexation secured health and safety for the Bartlesville residents rather than improving the accommodations of the Polish immigrants.[175]

This annexation of parts of Smeltertown combined with faltering of the smelting business to create an unfriendly environment for many of the Polish residents. This, in turn, caused a large Polish exodus from the area beginning in 1919. As previously stated, the city directories did not list all Polish people, undercutting the population of poor and working-class immigrants. However, the numbers do reveal the mass departure of Polish citizens. The 1917 city directory listed 119 people of Polish background. In 1919, it had fallen to 91, and in 1920, it again fell to 39.[176] In 1921, the three zinc smelters closed due to a reduction in production of the tri-state mining district. Only National Zinc reopened in 1922, but by then, the number of Polish immigrants in the directory numbered only 17.[177]

Chapter 6

OKLAHOMA DOUGHBOYS

BASIL D. HARTER of Oklahoma City served in Company A, 315th Engineers, 90th Division, traveling overseas on June 14, 1918. He participated in the St. Mihiel and Meuse-Argonne Offensives before serving in the Army of Occupation in Germany. He returned to the United States on July 7, 1919.

Basil D. Harter. *Author's collection.*

BEN VAN GUNDA of Miami, Oklahoma, served with Company F, 115th Infantry, 29th Division, going overseas on June 15, 1918. He participated in the Meuse-Argonne Offensive and returned to the United States on May 24, 1919. He received the Distinguished Service Cross and Croix de Guerre with palm for actions while serving as a Chauchaut automatic rifleman.

During the early phases of the Meuse-Argonne Offensive, while in the Bois de Consenvoye, Van Gunda operated his rifle in single opposition to multiple German advances. He held the line until American reinforcements could join his defense. For this action, he received the Distinguished Service Cross.

Ben Van Gunda. *Author's collection.*

Van Gunda received his Croix de Guerre for actions while advancing against three concrete machine gun nests that constantly harassed the American drive. Van Gunda crawled out into the open and suddenly stood up to draw their fire. Once he learned their positions, he led attacks against them and eliminated the positions.[178]

Harry Hunter of Tulsa, Oklahoma, served in Company I, 51st Infantry, 6th Division, and went overseas on July 6, 1918. He participated in the fighting in the Gerardmer Sector and in the Meuse-Argonne Offensive. He was attached to the 3rd Battalion Scouts and gained a reputation as one "with nerve and ability."

Jack B. Eisenhart of Oklahoma City served in Company H, 353rd Infantry, 89th Division. He was wounded by artillery around August 26, 1918, and sent to the hospital, where he recovered and rejoined his unit in the Army of Occupation.

Left: Harry Hunter. *Author's collection.*

Right: Jack B. Eisenhart. *Author's collection.*

Left: John D. Wilhoit. *Courtesy of Bruce Jarvis.*

Right: Joseph F. Kupka. *Author's collection.*

JOHN DOUGLASS WILHOIT of Chickasha, Oklahoma, served in Company L, 112th Infantry, 28th Division. He went overseas on May 7, 1918, and participated in the Battles of Champagne, Champagne-Marne, Aisne-Marne, Oise-Marne, Lorraine and Meuse-Argonne. He returned to the United States on April 30, 1919.

JOSEPH F. KUPKA of Canute, Oklahoma, was an Austrian immigrant. He served in the Conservation and Reclamation Depot 301, Quartermaster Corps, going overseas on September 23, 1918.

WILLIAM P. ERWIN of Ryan, Oklahoma, enlisted in the Aviation Section of the U.S. Army Signal Corps in April 1917. On July 19, 1918, he was assigned to the 1st Observation Squadron and quickly became one of the greatest aviators of the war. He was credited with destroying eight enemy aircraft and performing several great acts of valor for which he was awarded the Distinguished Service Cross and the French Croix de Guerre.

William P. Erwin. *Courtesy of Chuck Thomas.*

His Croix de Guerre citation reads: "On 20 July 1918, he volunteered for an infantry liaison mission at night fall, executed this mission at 200 meters altitude. He brought back his observer, who was mortally wounded, and his plane was full of bullet holes."

His Distinguished Service Cross citations reads:

The Distinguished Service Cross is presented to William P. Erwin, First Lieutenant (Air Service), U.S. Army, for extraordinary heroism in action in the Chateau-Thierry and St. Mihiel Salients, France. Lieutenant Erwin, with Second Lieutenant Byrne E. Baucom, observer, by a long period of faithful and heroic operations, set an inspiring example of courage and devotion to duty to his entire squadron. Throughout the Chateau-Thierry actions, in June and July, 1918, he flew under the worst weather conditions and successfully carried out his missions in the face of heavy odds. In the St. Mihiel sector, September 12–15, 1918, he repeated his previous courageous work. He flew as low as 50 feet from the ground behind the enemy's lines, harassing German troops with machine-gun fire and subjecting himself to attack from ground batteries, machine-guns, and rifles. He twice drove off enemy planes which were attempting to destroy an American observation balloon. On September 12 and 13, 1918, he flew at extremely low altitudes and carried out infantry contact patrols successfully. Again, on September 12 he attacked a German battery, forced the crew to abandon it, shot off of his horse a German officer who was trying to escape, drove the cannoneers to their dugouts, and kept them there until the infantry could come up and capture them.

He remained in the Army Air Service after the war.

PVT. ALEX K. ADWAN
HEALDTON   W.A.

Left: Alex Adwan. *From* Soldiers of the Great War, *vol. 3 (1920).*

Right: Fred Beardsley. *Author's collection.*

ALEX ADWAN of Healdton, Oklahoma, immigrated to Oklahoma from Syria as a child. He served in the Machine Gun Company, 357th Infantry, 90th Division, going overseas on June 20, 1918. He participated in the St. Mihiel and Meuse-Argonne Offensives. During an attack on October 24, 1918, in the Argonne forest on "Dead Man's Hill," his machine gun emplacement suffered a direct hit of a German artillery shell. Although fatally wounded, he managed to walk seven miles to a hospital, where he eventually died on November 5, 1918.[179]

FRED V. BEARDSLEY of Snyder, Oklahoma, served with Company A, 49th Engineers, and worked on railways in France. He went overseas on July 9, 1918, and returned to the United States on July 7, 1919.

Left: Alvin Ragsdale. *Courtesy of the Ragsdale family.*

Right: Clyde Ragsdale. *Courtesy of the Ragsdale family.*

ALVIN RAGSDALE of Oklahoma City served in Company O, 5th Battalion 22nd Engineers, Light Railways. While in France, he participated in the Meuse-Argonne Offensive.

CLYDE RAGSDALE of Oklahoma City served in Company F, 142nd Infantry, 36th Division. He participated in the Meuse-Argonne Offensive.

JAMES TEEL of Bartlesville served in Company E, 358th Infantry, 90th Division. During the St. Mihiel Offensive, on September 12, 1918, Teel was killed by a machine gun while leading his platoon forward.[180] The American Legion honored Teel by naming American Legion Post 105 after him.

PHYLETUS REED of Ochelata served with the Machine Gun Company, 358th Infantry, 90th Division. He was killed in action on September 22, 1918, during the St. Mihiel Offensive.

Phyletus Reed
Died 9-22-1918

Above, left: James Teel. *Courtesy of the Bartlesville Historical Society.*

Above, right: Phyletus Reed. *Courtesy of the Bartlesville Historical Society.*

Left: Vernon Parker. *Courtesy of the Bartlesville Historical Society.*

Vernie R. Parker

VERNON PARKER of Dewey, Oklahoma, served with the 13th Evacuation Hospital, U.S. Army, in Vladivostok, Russia. He died of disease on May 3, 1919.

GLENN CONDON of Tulsa, Oklahoma, served as the chairman of the Four Minute Men for the State of Oklahoma. Under his leadership, practically every county in the state had a successful program wherein speakers would give four-minute patriotic speeches to encourage the community to support the war effort. In December 1917, he accompanied his sister-in-law Cora Youngblood Corson overseas to gather firsthand accounts of the war to bring back to the people of Oklahoma. Condon traveled to France and spent several weeks touring the front lines and gathering souvenirs. Upon his return to the United States, he toured Oklahoma

Glenn Condon. *Author's collection.*

showing his souvenirs and captivating audiences with his experiences. However, Condon felt he could do more, so on July 13, 1918, he joined the United States Marine Corps. Due to his experience with the Four Minute Men and his service in Oklahoma's state legislature, he was immediately placed into the Marine Corps Recruiting Publicity Bureau in New York City. He received his discharge in 1919.

CORA YOUNGBLOOD CORSON of Anadarko, Oklahoma, was one of the most popular vaudeville performers in the United States for many years. However, once the country went to war, she focused her energy on publicly supporting the war effort. In December 1917, she took her group, the Cora Youngblood Corson Instrumentalists, overseas to Europe in order to entertain the troops. Once in the United Kingdom, the group planned to tour for six months but ended up fully booked for a year and four months throughout England and Ireland. During this time, they performed more than sixty concerts for sick and wounded soldiers.[181] They even performed through German air raids in London, with shrapnel from a bomb damaging Cora's tuba. After the war ended on November 11, 1918, Cora Youngblood Corson and her Instrumentalists performed for President Woodrow Wilson during his trip to Manchester on December 30.[182]

On May 4, 1919, Cora and her band traveled to La Havre, France, and joined the Knights of Columbus under the name the Knights of

Cora Youngblood Corson. *Author's collection.*

Columbus Troubadours. They were the only women to perform as part of the organization, and they traveled across France and into occupied Germany to play shows for soldiers. During their time overseas, they reportedly performed for over one million Allied soldiers in France, seventy-five thousand in Germany and ten thousand men of the U.S. Navy in the harbors of Europe. On August 12, 1919, Cora and her group sailed home for the United States.[183]

Left: Myatt Myatt. *Courtesy of the Stillwater History Museum.*

Right: The Vrana brothers: William (*left*), Peter (*center*), Edmond (*right*). *From* The Oklahoma Spirit of '17.

MYATT WILLIAM MYATT of Yale, Oklahoma, enlisted in the army on May 24, 1918. He went overseas on August 14, 1918, with the Motor Truck Company No. 455, Motor Supply Train No. 415, Quartermaster Corps, which operated under the 3rd Corps. He participated in the occupation of Germany and received a discharge in August 1919.

WILLIAM VRANA of Oklahoma City served overseas in the 111th Ammunition Train, 36th Division. He participated in the St. Mihiel and Meuse-Argonne Offensives. He received his discharge on June 18, 1919.[184]

EDMOND VRANA of Oklahoma City entered service on June 30, 1917. He served in Company C, 142nd Infantry, 36th Division, and sailed overseas in July 1918. He participated in the Meuse-Argonne Offensive. On October 9, 1918, he was killed by an explosive shell.[185]

PETER VRANA of Oklahoma City entered service on June 30, 1917, and served overseas with Company G, 324th Infantry, 81st Division. He participated in the Meuse-Argonne Offensive. He received his discharge in July 1919.[186]

MARTIN BOETTGER of Oklahoma City entered service in September 1917. He joined Company E, 110th Infantry, 28th Division, and fought in the St. Mihiel and Meuse-Argonne Offensives. On October 1, 1918, Boettger was killed in action while delivering a message near the town of Apremont.[187]

ROYDEN BALDWIN of Oklahoma City entered service on November 20, 1917. He received training at Fort Logan and joined Company L, 31st Infantry. He traveled overseas on June 5, 1918, but instead of traveling to France, he crossed the Pacific and landed in the Philippines. The 31st then traveled to Siberia, where he defended the Trans-Siberian Railway from Russian combatants. He received his discharge on October 9, 1919.[188]

Left: Martin Boettger. *From* The Oklahoma Spirit of '17.

Right: Royden Baldwin and Elizabeth Miller. *From* The Oklahoma Spirit of '17.

Elizabeth L. Miller of Oklahoma City entered service on September 17, 1918, and received training at Camp Dodge at U.S. Government Medical Corps Hospital 21 in Denver, Colorado. She served with the Red Cross through the war. She was discharged on November 12, 1919.[189]

Artie E. Brown of Choctaw, Oklahoma, entered service on April 1, 1917. He trained with Company M, Oklahoma National Guard, at Fort Sill before being transferred to Company F, 142nd Infantry, 36th Division. He went overseas on July 10, 1918, and was killed on October 9, 1918. He was shot in the arm by a machine gun bullet and bled out.[190] He posthumously received the Croix de Guerre. His citation read: "During the combats near St. Etienne…he displayed extraordinary heroism. Was killed in the course of the action."

Artie E. Brown. *From* The Oklahoma Spirit of '17.

Jessie C. Sampson of Watonga, Oklahoma, entered service in April 1917. He trained at the Great Lakes Station and joined the USS *Tyler*. He embarked overseas in March 1918, landing in Italy. During the ship's return trip to the United States, it was torpedoed on May 2, 1918. Sampson was killed by the explosion.[191] However, before his death, he flaunted the Stars and Stripes in the face of the German submarine. A letter from Secretary of the Navy Josephus Daniels to Jessie's mother read:

> *The department has received a detailed report of the sinking of the S.S.* Tyler, *in which your son, Jessie C. Sampson, lost his life.*
> *The armed guard commander of the S.S.* Tyler *has brought to the special attention of the department the splendid behavior of the after gun crew, who stood at their posts until the ship was shattered. Your son, Jessie C. Sampson,*

Jessie Sampson. *From* The Oklahoma Spirit of '17.

was a member of this gun crew, and as soon as there was evidence that an engagement would take place with the enemy, hoisted the colors. Shortly after this the young man was blown from the after gun platform by the force of the torpedo's explosion and was killed.

The department feels that you can well feel proud of your son who so gallantly gave up his life in the face of the enemy.[192]

Lonnie A. Hill. *From* The Oklahoma Spirit of '17.

LONNIE A. HILL of Chickasha entered service on August 4, 1917, and served with Company D, 142nd Infantry, 36th Division. He went overseas in July 1918. On October 9, 1918, near St. Etienne, Hill assisted an ammunition carrier, but as he stepped out of his dugout, a high explosive round landed nearby, mortally wounding him. He died shortly thereafter.[193] He posthumously received a Croix de Guerre with Palm for his actions. His citation stated:

For extraordinary heroism in action near St. Etienne, France, October 8, 1918. The advance made by Corporal Hill was out into open field, under heavy shell and machine gun fire, succeeding, with the help of his comrades, in taking enemy positions. While in the advance, he was struck by enemy shells, from which wounds he died.

Leo LeBron. *From* The Oklahoma Spirit of '17.

LEO PARROTT LEBRON of Oklahoma City worked for the Fort Smith and Western Railway Company. He entered service on August 6, 1917, and was commissioned as a captain. He sailed for France with the Casual Engineers on January 23, 1918, aboard the U.S. Transport *Tuscania*. On February 5, 1918, while off the Irish coast, a German U-boat torpedoed the *Tuscania*, sinking it with a loss of 210 men, including Leo Lebron. He became the first Oklahoma officer killed in war.[194]

CHESTER ARTHUR HIRSCHI of Guthrie, Oklahoma, joined the service on April 26, 1918, and was assigned to Company I, 357th Infantry, 90th Division. He sailed overseas on June 20, 1918. He participated in the St. Mihiel and Meuse-Argonne Offensives. On October 23, 1918, while attempting to take the town of Bantheville, Hirschi was killed in action.[195]

RALPH C. JOHNSON of Guthrie, Oklahoma, enlisted in the U.S. Marine Corps on August 3, 1917. On April 1, 1918, he joined the 74th Company, 6th Regiment, 4th Brigade (Marine), in the trenches around Verdun. On the night of April 12, the 74th Company slept in reserve at Camp Fontaine–St. Robert. The Germans unleashed a heavy barrage of explosives and gas that flooded the area, catching the marines asleep.[196] All officers of the 74th had to be evacuated, and around 220 men were burned or inhaled the gas, with 40 dying as a result. Johnson was evacuated to the hospital but succumbed to gas poisoning on April 29.[197]

WILLIAM A. EDWARDS of Crescent, Oklahoma, joined the service on January 8, 1918, and was sent to the Philippines to train with Company D, 31st Infantry, 81st Division. On March 5, 1918, he sailed from the tropics to the frigid cold of Siberia to prevent Allied war material from being looted from Vladivostok and guard the Trans-Siberian Railroad. His unit saw action against Russian troops throughout Siberia. Edwards returned to the United States and received his discharge on January 12, 1920.[198]

ELOISE EAGLETON of Norman, Oklahoma, attended school in Pawnee, Oklahoma, and the University of Oklahoma, where she received a BA and MA. During the war, she served as secretary of the YWCA at the University of Oklahoma for two years and performed war work as the chairman of the Canteen Committee in Norman. She died of influenza on October 18, 1918.[199]

WILLIAM L. EAGLETON of Norman, Oklahoma, brother of Eloise Eagleton, was attending the law school at the University of Oklahoma when he entered service on May 11, 1917. He went to officers' training school and was commissioned as a second lieutenant. He went overseas on July 21, 1918,

Clockwise from top left: Chester Hirschi; Ralph Johnson; Eloise Eagleton; William Edwards. *From* The Oklahoma Spirit of '17.

and eventually attached to Battery D, 129th Field Artillery, 35th Division. He fought in the St. Mihiel and Meuse-Argonne Offensives. Eagleton caught influenza but recovered and returned home on March 10, 1919, and was discharged on March 22, 1919, at Camp Upton.[200]

WILLIS LEROY PEARCE of Ardmore, Oklahoma, was born in Smith Center, Kansas; educated in the Agricultural College at Manhattan, Kansas; and joined the National Guard in 1904. He rose from private to captain of Company I, 1st Kansas, in 1915 and served on the Mexican border in 1916. After returning home, he transferred into the reserves and moved to Ardmore, Oklahoma. He again entered military service on January 21, 1918. He received a captain's commission on April 19 and commanded Company F, 142nd Infantry, 36th Division. On October 8, 1918, while leading his men during the fighting around St. Etienne, he was wounded by a machine gun in the chest but bandaged it up and led his company forward. However, the blood loss soon became too much, and he was forced to withdraw to the rear. While he was returning to American lines, an enemy shell struck nearby, killing him.[201] He received the French Croix de Guerre for his actions.[202]

Left: William Eagleton. *Right*: Willis Pearce. *From* The Oklahoma Spirit of '17.

Left: Earl Hignight. *Right*: Dick Breeding. *From* The Oklahoma Spirit of '17.

EARL K. HIGNIGHT of Ardmore, Oklahoma, joined the National Guard in 1916 during the Mexican Border War and served on the border in Texas. He remained in the National Guard after federalization and joined Company E, 142nd Infantry, 36th Division. Hignight sailed overseas on July 18, 1918. On October 8, 1918, during the fighting around St. Etienne, he was killed in action.[203]

DICK B. BREEDING was born in Seminole, Oklahoma, educated in Holdenville and attended the University of Oklahoma in Norman. He enlisted in the army in 1916 and served during the Mexican Border War. He returned from Mexico in March 1917 but reentered the army in April, being assigned to Fort Sill for training with Company A, 167th Infantry, 42nd Division. He attended officers' training school at Leon Springs, Texas, and was commissioned a second lieutenant. In October 1917, he married Frankie Riley in New York before going overseas in November 1917 with Company A. Breeding received the Distinguished Service Cross for actions on May 12, 1918, for *extraordinary heroism in action at Vacqueville, France, May 12ᵗʰ, 1918. Lieutenant Breeding had been out with a patrol into the enemy's lines when it was discovered that one member of the patrol was missing. Lieutenant Breeding with another officer volunteered to return into the enemy lines in search of the missing man, thereby setting an example of determination, energy, and bravery. They proceeded on their mission and, while looking for the missing man discovered one of the enemy lurking in the bushes, whereupon Lieutenant Breeding shot and killed him, bringing the body into the American lines. Valuable information was obtained which aided materially in the later action of the command.*

During the Battle of Chateau Thierry, he received the French Croix de Guerre. On July 26, 1918, he was killed in action during an attack on enemy-held positions southwest of La Croix Rouge Ferme near Beuvardes, France.[204]

GILBERT MOORE of Holdenville, Oklahoma, enlisted in the National Guard in May 1917. His father, G.L. Moore, had served in the Spanish-American War, and Gilbert sought to continue the tradition of service. Moore traveled to Camp Bowie, Texas, to train with Company F, 142ⁿᵈ Infantry, 36ᵗʰ Division. He went overseas on July 18, 1918. On October 8, 1918, while fighting at Blanc Mont Ridge, Moore "got up and started out toward a machine gun nest, when he was hit by machine gun bullet in the right kidney, killing him instantly."[205] He received the Croix de Guerre for actions.[206]

LESLIE E. CORN of Okmulgee was born in Illinois but moved to Oklahoma as a young child. He enlisted in the U.S. Marine Corps on June 13, 1917. He served in the 95ᵗʰ Company, 6ᵗʰ Regiment, 4ᵗʰ Brigade (Marines), in France. He fought in the trenches of Verdun with the 2ⁿᵈ Division and the brutal combat of Belleau Wood, where he died of wounds received in combat on June 12, 1918.[207]

JOSEPH CLEMENT MASON of Grayhorse, Oklahoma, a member of the Osage Nation, was educated at the Chilocco Indian Agricultural School. He entered the service on February 25, 1918, and trained at Camp Travis with the Field Remount Guard 306. He went overseas on June 30, 1918, and returned to the United States on June 17, 1919.[208]

Above, left: Gilbert Moore. *Above, right*: Leslie Corn. *Left*: Joseph C. Mason. *From* The Oklahoma Spirit of '17.

Left: Charles Choteau. *Right*: John Yellowhorse. *From* The Oklahoma Spirit of '17.

CHARLES CHOTEAU of Pawhuska, Oklahoma, was a member of the Osage Nation. He served in Company E, 142nd Infantry, 36th Division, an all-Indian company. He participated in the intense fighting at St. Etienne near Blanc Mont Ridge. He received his discharge at Camp Pike on June 14, 1919.[209]

JOHN YELLOWHORSE of Fairfax, Oklahoma, was a member of the Osage Nation. He trained at Camp Travis with the 41st Division before going overseas with the Camp Pike September Automatic Replacement Draft Company 24 on September 30, 1918. He served with the Depot Service Company 36 in France until August 30, 1919. During the war, his infant child died after a short illness on June 24, 1918.[210] Yellowhorse received his discharge at Camp Pike in September 1919.[211]

Barney E. Kinney. *From* The Oklahoma Spirit of '17.

BARNEY EARNEST KINNEY of Paoli, Oklahoma, was born in Texas in 1895 but moved to Oklahoma as a child with his family. He enlisted in the U.S. Marine Corps on February 14, 1918. He trained at Mare Island, California, until May 11, when he joined Casual Company, Replacement Battalion. On June 22, he joined the 23rd Machine Gun Company (B), 6th Machine Gun Battalion (USMC), in France as a replacement from the intense fighting at Belleau Wood. He then participated in the Battles of Soissons, St. Mihiel, Blanc Mont, Ridge and the Meuse-Argonne Offensive. On the night of November 10, just a few hours before the armistice would end the war, Kinney was killed by shell fire in the Argonne Forest while attempting to cross the Meuse River.[212]

THE STORIES REFLECTED in this book tell of the sacrifices made by the men and women of Oklahoma during World War I. The stories of the doughboys reflect the thousands of men who served their country at home and overseas. They all served their country when called on, and we remember their service. The actions of Oklahomans helped end the war and cement the legacy of the state in the history of the war.

NOTES

Prologue

1. Clarence C. Clendenen, *Blood on the Border: The United States Army and the Mexican Irregulars* (London, 1969), 285–98.
2. Texas Military Forces Museum, "36th Division in World War I," www.texasmilitaryforcesmuseum.org/36division/archives/wwi/white/chap1.htm.

Chapter 1

3. W.E. Welch, J.S. Aldridge and L.V. Aldridge, *The Oklahoma Spirit of '17* (Oklahoma City, OK: Historical Publishing Co., 1920), 412–13.
4. Mitch Meador, "A Look Back at Fort Sill's Early Aviation Days," U.S. Army, August 9, 2018, www.army.mil/article/209676/a_look_back_at_fort_sills_early_aviation_days
5. Ibid.
6. Unnamed photo album, in author's possession.
7. *The Thirty-Sixth Division in the Great War* (France, 1919), 5–10.
8. George Wythe, *History of the 90th Division* (Ninetieth Division Association, 1920), 3–196.

Chapter 2

9. Bertha Hale White, "The Green Corn Rebellion in Oklahoma," *The New Day* 4, no. 9 (March 4, 1922): 68.

10. Nigel Anthony Sellars, *Oil, Wheat, and Wobblies: The Industrial Workers of the World in Oklahoma, 1905–1930* (Norman: University of Oklahoma Press, 1998), 80.

11. James Weinstein, *The Decline of American Socialism, 1912–1925* (New York: Monthly Review Press, 1967), 139.

12. *Okemah Ledger*, "Troop A Takes a Hand," August 9, 1917, 1.

13. *Okemah Ledger*, "Hughes and Seminole Counties in Open Revolt," August 9, 1917, 1.

14. Sellars, *Oil, Wheat, and Wobblies*, 90–91.

15. *Daily Oklahoman*, "200 Creeks Go On Warpath over Drafting of Youths; 3 Whites Rumored Killed," June 6, 1918.

16. *Chickasha Daily Express*, "Outbreak Now Seems Huge Joke," June 6, 1918.

17. Ellen Perryman to Guy O. Taylor, Five Tribes, CCF, 1907–39, Records of the Bureau of Indian Affairs, Record Group 75, National Archives, Washington, D.C. (hereafter cited as RG 75, NA); *Tulsa Democrat*, "Indian Rebellion Simmers Down to Minor Discontent," June 6, 1918; *McAlester News*, "Creek Indians Tell of Recent Tribe Troubles," June 8, 1918.

18. *Henryetta Free-Lance*, "Misunderstanding Creates Passion for Resistance," June 7, 1918.

19. *Henryetta Standard*, "Must Have Flour Card," June 6, 1918.

20. *Henryetta Free-Lance*, "Misunderstanding Creates Passion."

21. *Oklahoma News*, "Negroes Who Want Flour in 'Revolt,'" June 6, 1918.

22. Thomas Britten, *American Indians in World War I: At War and at Home* (Albuquerque: University of New Mexico Press, 1997), 51, 53.

23. Ibid.

24. *Wichita Daily Eagle*, "Creek Indians Rebel Against Draft Rulings," June 6, 1918.

25. Ibid.

26. Affidavit of Jack Carter, June 22, 1918, RG 75, NA.

27. Tulsay to John McElroy, June 6, 1918, Five Tribes, CCF, 1907–39, RBIA, RG 75, NA.

28. *Henryetta Free-Lance*, "Misunderstanding Creates Passion."

29. Affidavit of Jack Carter, June 22, 1918, Five Tribes, CCF, 1907–39, RBIA, RG 75, NA.

30. Ibid.

31. Harry B. Sedicum to Gabe Parker, June 15, 1918, Five Tribes, CCF, 1907–39, RBIA, RG 75, NA.
32. Tulsay to John McElroy, June 6, 1918, Five Tribes, CCF, 1907–39, RBIA, RG 75, NA.
33. Ellen Perryman to Guy O. Taylor, Five Tribes, CCF, 1907–39, RBIA, RG 75, NA.
34. Harry B. Sedicum to Gabe Parker, June 15, 1918, Five Tribes, CCF, 1907–39, RBIA, RG 75, NA.
35. *Paris Morning News*, "Posse Goes after Alleged Disloyal Indian Woman," June 7, 1918.
36. *Tulsa Democrat*, "Indian Rebellion Simmers Down to Minor Discontent," June 6, 1918.
37. *Henryetta Free-Lance*, "Misunderstanding Creates Passion."
38. *McAlester News-Capital*, "Creek Indians Tell of Recent Tribe Troubles," June 8, 1918.
39. *Henryetta Free-Lance*, "Misunderstanding Creates Passion."
40. *The Sun*, "Indians Rebel at Army Draft Under German Influence," June 6, 1918.
41. Ibid.
42. *New York Times*, "Creek Indians Rise Against the Draft: Three Whites Reported Killed in Oklahoma – Pro-German Plot Is Blamed," June 6, 1918.
43. *Daily Oklahoman*, "200 Creeks Go On Warpath."
44. *The Sun*, "That Creek Indian Uprising Now Denied," June 11, 1918.
45. *Muskogee Daily Phoenix*, "One hundred Creek Indians…," June 16, 1918.
46. *Henryetta Standard*, "It looks as though…," June 6, 1918.
47. *Henryetta Free-Lance*, "Misunderstanding Creates Passion."
48. Jerry Rand to H.B. Pears, July 27, 1918, Five Tribes, CCF, 1907–39, RBIA, RG 75, NA.
49. H.B. Pears to Cato Sells, August 22, 1918, Five Tribes, CCF, 1907–39, RBIA, RG 75, NA.
50. *Henryetta Free-Lance*, "Misunderstanding Creates Passion."
51. *Daily Oklahoman*, "200 Creeks Go On Warpath."
52. *El Paso Times*, "Oklahoma Home Guards Called Out to Quell Indian Anti-Draft Riots," June 6, 1918.
53. *Norwich Bulletin*, "700 Creek Indians Have Taken Refuge in Hills," June 6, 1918.
54. *Morning Tulsa Daily World*, "Creek Indians Are Reported in Rebellion Against Draft," June 6, 1918.

55. MaryAnn Weston, *Native Americans in the News: Images of Indians in the Twentieth Century Press* (Westport, CT: Praeger Publishers, 1996), 2.

56. *New York Times*, "Creek Indians Rise Against the Draft."

57. *The Sun*, "Indians Rebel at Army Draft Under German Influence," June 6, 1918.

58. *Wilmington Morning Star*, "Creek Indians Revolt Against Draft—Result of German Propaganda," June 6, 1918.

59. H.B. Peairs to Cato Sells, July 6, 1918, Five Tribes, CCF, 1907–39, RBIA, RG 75, NA.

60. Gabe Parker to Cato Sells, September 16, 1918, Five Tribes, CCF, 1907–39, RBIA, RG 75, NA.

61. *America in Europe*, "The Creek Indians in Revolt," July 29. 1918, Enemy Activities—Propaganda 1917–18, American Unofficial Collection of World War I Photographs 1917–18, Record Group 165: Records of the War Department General and Special Staffs, 1860–1952, National Archives.

62. *The Native American*, "Indian Soldiers," 19 (June 1918): 170.

63. Geoffrey R. Stone, *Perilous Times: Free Speech in Wartime from the Sedition Act of 1798 to the War on Terrorism* (New York: W.W. Norton & Company, 2004), 12.

64. Gabe Parker to Cato Sells, June 11, 1918, Five Tribes, CCF, 1907–39, RBIA, RG 75, NA.

65. Thomas Britten, "The Creek Draft Rebellion of 1918," *Chronicles of Oklahoma* (Summer 2001): 205.

66. Harry B. Sedicum to Gabe Parker, June 15, 1918, Five Tribes, CCF, 1907–39, RBIA, RG 75, NA.

67. Carl J. O'Hornett to Gabe Parker, June 17, 1918, Five Tribes, CCF, 1907–39, RBIA, RG 75, NA.

68. Gabe Parker to Harry Sedicum, June 19, 1918, Five Tribes, CCF, 1907–39, RBIA, RG 75, NA.

69. Gabe Parker to Cato Sells, June 20, 1918, Five Tribes, CCF, 1907–39, RBIA, RG 75, NA.

70. H.B. Peairs to Cato Sells, July 6, 1918, Five Tribes, CCF, 1907–39, RBIA, RG 75, NA.

71. Britten, "Creek Draft Rebellion of 1918," 207.

72. W.L. Reed to James C. Davis, August 10, 1918, Five Tribes, CCF, 1907–39, RBIA, RG 75, NA.

73. Ibid.

74. James C. Davis to Gabe Parker, August 10, 1918, Five Tribes, CCF, 1907–39, RBIA, RG 75, NA.

75. H.B. Peairs to Cato Sells, August 22, 1918, Five Tribes, CCF, 1907–39, RBIA, RG 75, NA.

76. E.J. Burke to Gabe Parker, Five Tribes, CCF, 1907–39, RBIA, RG 75, NA.

77. Letter to A. Bruce Bielaski, September 11, 1918, Five Tribes, CCF, 1907–39, RBIA, RG 75, NA.

78. H.A. Archer to Gabe Parker, September 24, 1918, Five Tribes, CCF, 1907–39, RBIA, RG 75, NA.

79. Willis W. Christopher to Treasury Department Secret Service Division, October 22, 1918, Five Tribes, CCF, 1907–39, RBIA, RG 75, NA.

80. *Muskogee Daily Phoenix*, "Officers Cuffed by Indian Woman," December 12, 1918.

81. James C. Davis to Cato Sells, December 18, 1918, Five Tribes, CCF, 1907–39, RBIA, RG 75, NA.

Chapter 3

82. "Letter from Governor R.L. Williams to Water Hert," July 21, 1917, in author's possession.

83. "Letter from J.M. Aydelato to W.L. Hert," August 1, 1917, in author's possession.

84. "Oklahoma Council of Defense," *Encyclopedia of Oklahoma History and Culture*, www.okhistory.org/publications/enc/entry.php?entry=OK038.

85. James H. Fowler II, "Tar and Feather Patriotism: The Suppression of Dissent in Oklahoma During World War One," *Chronicles of Oklahoma* 56, no. 4 (Winter 1978–79): 409.

86. "Letter to the Pawnee County Council of Defense from the Payne County Council of Defense," April 17, 1918, Stillwater History Museum.

87. "Letter to the Payne County Council of Defense," April 24, 1918, Stillwater History Museum.

88. "Letter to the First National Bank from the Payne County Council of Defense," April 24, 1918, Stillwater History Museum.

89. Oklahoma State Council of Defense, *Sooners in the War* (Oklahoma City, 1919), 31–32.

90. *Harlow's Weekly* (Oklahoma City, Oklahoma), "Some Sections…," June 19, 1918, 9.

91. *Cordell Beacon*, "Anti-German Order Causes Trouble," October 10, 1918, 1.
92. David Levy, "The University of Oklahoma and World War I," *Chronicles of Oklahoma* (Summer 2006): 136.
93. Spirit of Oklahoma, 414.
94. Levy, "University of Oklahoma and World War I," 135.
95. Ibid., 140.
96. Ibid., 141.
97. Ibid., 143.
98. Ibid., 144.
99. Ibid., 145–46.
100. Ibid., 147.
101. Ibid., 147–48.
102. Michael Casey, "The Closing of Cordell Christian College," *Chronicles of Oklahoma* (Spring 1998): 21.
103. Ibid., 23.
104. Ibid., 24.
105. Ibid., 24–25.
106. Ibid., 25–27.
107. Ibid., 28.
108. Ibid., 29.
109. Ibid., 30–31.
110. Ibid., 32, 35.
111. Charles W. Smith, "The Selling of America in Oklahoma: The First and Second Liberty Bond Drives," *Chronicles of Oklahoma* (Winter 1995): 439–40.
112. Ibid., 442.
113. Ibid., 443.
114. Ibid., 444–45.
115. *Daily Oklahoman*, "Are You Helping or Hurting Cause," June 14, 1917, 6.
116. Smith, "Selling of America in Oklahoma," 448.
117. Ibid., 449.

Chapter 4

118. Jason Herbert, "That I Might Render Account of Myself and People: Cherokees and World War I," *Chronicles of Oklahoma* (Spring 2017): 47.
119. Ibid., 50.

120. Ibid.

121. Ibid., 53.

122. Ibid., 53–54.

123. Ibid., 54.

124. Ibid., 60.

125. Ibid.

126. Susan Applegate Krouse, *North American Indians in the Great War* (Lincoln: University of Nebraska Press, 2007), 69.

127. Ibid., 57.

128. *Muskogee Times-Democrat*, "Indian Troupe Busy at Front," May 26, 1919, 3.

129. Herbert, "That I Might Render Account of Myself and People," 66.

Chapter 5

130. *McAlester News-Capital*, "Flu Took Heavy Toll in Lives," January 31, 1919, 1.

131. John M. Barry, *The Great Influenza* (New York: Penguin Books, 2005), 152, 231–32.

132. Ibid., 187–89, 224, 235–40.

133. "The Spanish Influenza Pandemic in Oklahoma City," www.metrolibrary.org/archives/essay/2019/07/spanish-influenza-pandemic-oklahoma-city.

134. Ibid.

135. Ibid.

136. Ibid.

137. Ibid.

138. *Morning Examiner*, "Growing Pains," May 7, 1918.

139. U.S. Department of Commerce, Bureau of the Census, *Sixteenth Census of the United States, 1940: Population*, Oklahoma, Table 2, 862.

140. Margaret Withers Teague, *History of Washington County and Surrounding Area*, vol. 2 (Bartlesville Historical Commission, 1968), 233.

141. *Washington County Sentinel and the Weekly Enterprise*, "Grand Opening Lot Sale," April 27, 1917.

142. Nigel Sellars, "The 1918 Spanish Flu Epidemic in Oklahoma," *Chronicles of Oklahoma* 79, no. 1 (Spring 2001): 37.

143. Nigel Anthony Sellars, "Almost Hopeless in the Wake of the Storm," *Chronicles of Oklahoma* 79 (Spring 2001): 48.

144. *Daily Oklahoman*, "City Has First Case of Flu," September 29, 1918.

145. *Morning Examiner*, "Nurses Needed to Fight the Influenza Epidemic," October 4, 1918

146. *Morning Examiner*, "Victim of Influenza," October 5, 1918, 5.

147. *Morning Examiner*, "Large Crowd Views the German War Trophies," October 6, 1918.

148. *Morning Examiner*, "City Schools Are Ordered Closed," October 8, 1918.

149. *Morning Examiner*, "Doctors Kept Busy by Victims of Influenza," October 8, 1918.

150. *Morning Examiner*, "Keep Children at Home," October 8, 1918.

151. *Morning Examiner*, "Open Flu Office," October 10, 1918.

152. *Morning Examiner*, "To Open Flu Hospital," October 12, 1918.

153. *Morning Examiner*, "Emergency Hospital Is Opened," October 13, 1918.

154. *Morning Examiner*, "Flu Epidemic Spreading Here," October 15, 1918.

155. Ibid.

156. Floyd Trippet, "Teenage to Old Age" (unpublished manuscript, 1971), 14.

157. Stanley Kazmierzak, oral interview by Richard Bernard, Bartlesville, Oklahoma, August 3, 1978.

158. *Morning Examiner*, "Orders West Side Clean-Up," October 13, 1918.

159. *Morning Examiner*, "Flu Increases 100 New Cases," October 16, 1918.

160. *Morning Examiner*, "Two Hospitals Are Kept Busy," October 17, 1918.

161. Ibid.

162. *Washington County Sentinel and the Weekly Enterprise*, "Time to Act," October 17, 1918.

163. Ibid.

164. *Morning Examiner*, "Flu Causes 10 Deaths," October 18, 1918.

165. *Morning Examiner*, "Force Pig Sty Cleanup," October 19, 1918.

166. *Morning Examiner*, "Deaths Are Fewer Now," October 20, 1918

167. *Morning Examiner*, "Negro Doctor Does His Bit," October 29, 1918.

168. *Morning Examiner*, "Order Pig Pens Removed," October 22, 1918.

169. *Morning Examiner*, "Scattered White Powder," October 22, 1918.

170. *Morning Examiner*, "White Powder Harmless," October 23, 1918.

171. *Morning Examiner*, "Guardsmen Aid Clean Up," October 23, 1918, 6.

172. Sellars, "Almost Hopeless in the Wake of the Storm," 48.

173. Richard M. Bernard, *The Poles in Oklahoma* (Norman: University of Oklahoma Press,1980), 62.

174. *Morning Examiner*, "City Takes in Addition," December 3, 1918.

175. *Bartlesville Daily Enterprise*, "Ordinance No. 846," January 6, 1919.

176. Bernard, *Poles in Oklahoma*, 52.
177. Teague, *History of Washington County*, 105–6.

Chapter 6

178. "Miami Soldier. Single Handed Captured Thirty-Three Germans," *Miami Record-Herald*, June 13, 1919, 2.
179. *Oklahoma News*, "Attend Hero's Funeral," July 30, 1921, 1.
180. *Morning Examiner*, "Sergt. Teel Died While Leading Men to Attack," February 14, 1919, 1.
181. *Cora Youngblood Corson Instrumentalists* brochure, author's collection.
182. "Cora Youngblood Corson's Instrumentalists Playing for President Wilson at Manchester," postcard, author's collection.
183. *The Girls from the Golden West* brochure, 1919, author's collection.
184. Welch, Aldridge and Aldridge, *Oklahoma Spirit of '17*, 33.
185. Ibid.
186. Ibid.
187. Ibid., 35.
188. Ibid., 37
189. Ibid.
190. Ibid., 44.
191. Ibid., 64.
192. *Watonga Republican*, "Former Watonga Boy Dies a Hero," September 12, 1918, 4.
193. Chaplain C.H. Barnes, *History of the 142nd Infantry of the Thirty-Sixth Division* (Blackwell Job Printing Company, 1922), 106–7.
194. Welch, Aldridge and Aldridge, *Oklahoma Spirit of '17*, 78.
195. Ibid., 79.
196. Major Edwin N. McClellan, "The Fourth Brigade of Marines in the Training Areas and the Operations in the Verdun Sector," *Marine Corps Gazette* 5, no. 1 (March 1920): 102.
197. Welch, Aldridge and Aldridge, *Oklahoma Spirit of '17*, 100.
198. Ibid., 110.
199. Ibid., 121.
200. Ibid.
201. *Daily Ardmoreite*, "Letters from Our Soldier Boys," February 9, 1919, 5.
202. Welch, Aldridge and Aldridge, *Oklahoma Spirit of '17*, 137.
203. Ibid., 141.

204. Ibid., 235.

205. Barnes, *History of the 142nd Infantry*, 119.

206. Welch, Aldridge and Aldridge, *Oklahoma Spirit of '17*, 236.

207. Ibid., 270.

208. Ibid., 307.

209. Ibid., 313.

210. *Osage Chief* (Fairfax, OK), "The infant child…," June 28, 1918, 3.

211. Welch, Aldridge and Aldridge, *Oklahoma Spirit of '17*, 320.

212. Ibid., 330.

ABOUT THE AUTHOR

James P. Gregory Jr. is a PhD candidate at the University of Oklahoma and is the director of the Louisiana State University Military History Museum. He is the author and editor of several books including *Unraveling the Myth of Sgt. Alvin York: The Other Sixteen*, *C'est la Guerre: The Memoir of Capt. James McBrayer Sellers, USMC*; *A Poet at War: The Story of a World War I Marine*; and *The Story of One Marine: The World War I Letters and Photos of Pvt. Thomas L. Stewart*.

Visit us at
www.historypress.com